The
Ragged Pursuit
of
Truth

Spinning
Pentecostal-Charismatic
Belief

RANDALL LEE

FriesenPress

Suite 300 - 990 Fort St
Victoria, BC, Canada, V8V 3K2
www.friesenpress.com

Copyright © 2015 by Randall Lee
First Edition — 2015

Unless otherwise noted, Scripture quotations are from the Holy Bible, New
International Version, Copyright © 1973, 1978, 1984 by International Bible Society.

ISBN
978-1-4602-7443-9 (Hardcover)
978-1-4602-7444-6 (Paperback)
978-1-4602-7445-3 (eBook)

1. Religion

Distributed to the trade by The Ingram Book Company

In gratitude to
my wife, Bonnie, a gift from God,
and partner in life and ministry:
You make me come up for air.

In remembrance of
Ray Levang (1920–1995),
his wonderful mind, his integrity and
his enlightening lectures on biblical hermeneutics.
A teacher and advisor.

Contents

Preface

My use of *Pentecostal-Charismatic* requires clarification. The High Church Charismatic who does not regard himself derived from common Pentecostal stock may see an unflattering inference. Not to worry—this book is not about him and he is not in the field of view. The contemporary mainstream Pentecostal who knows what being "Charismatic" suggests to him and does not like the implied association may similarly wince, but he too can relax. He is not on the radar.

I use the term *Pentecostal-Charismatic* to reference the very large and diverse company of Charismatic believers in general who, realizing it or not, and liking it or not, have a network of traceable roots to classical Pentecostalism. This comprises a broad band of significant denominations, church networks, local independent churches, home churches, miscellaneous pockets and innumerable free spirits. Many of these prefer "Charismatic" to distinguish themselves from mainline Pentecostal churches, but there is a common history. The DNA is not lying, and there are several strands of it.

Here one finds a bold identification between Holy Spirit baptism and speaking in unknown languages—and not just a doctrinal affirmation. These are ardent practitioners. Decades ago, zealous Pentecostals shifted into the formative Charismatic movement in great numbers. Many of them were pastors abandoning a mother ship they believed to be stuffy and languid. A younger generation, among them pastors' kids, youth pastors and college students, many steeped in evangelism and discipleship training, came with them. The timely arrival of them all brought much-needed order and direction to many sectors of an immature and turbulent Charismatic world. They also brought with them large doses of fervent Pentecostalism and many of their own ideas. Independent Pentecostal and fringe ministries found wide-open spaces and receptive ears. Some became leading Charismatic gurus, conference speakers, and authors. Novel teachings and "deeper truths," largely dismissed and shuffled to the Pentecostal periphery years before, also found fertile ground and greenhouse conditions in the broadly Charismatic frontier. They flourished, and their outlines can be seen today in the doctrinal baselines of many Charismatic constituencies.

Several Charismatic distinctives appear born of necessity and opportunity, and not imported, especially the early and pervasive investment in mentoring-discipleship, and a widespread preference for homegrown leadership. Charismatic worship caught everyone's attention and much of it was borrowed by a larger church world. Church structure is a constant on the horizon and governance models diverge from most of the major Pentecostal denominations. But even these disclose some Pentecostal roots of a bitter sort: former Pentecostals wary of district superintendents and pastors who were done with congregationally elected boards. Adaptations of the old Pentecostal Latter Rain paradigm, the fivefold ministry offices, are prolific throughout the movement, exposing yet another line of continuity. The Pentecostal-Charismatic handle is a keeper.

This book is not an overview of the Pentecostal-Charismatic world. It is not a travel guide. But it is a *travel advisory*, offering cautionary counsel and some warnings to unseasoned travellers. Much of what appears the same on the surface is not, and the Pentecostal-Charismatic world is not always a safe and healthy place. These chapters home in on a single dimension, namely the "mazing" world of Pentecostal-Charismatic theology and belief, how it is derived, what feeds it and how much of it ultimately reduces the lives of those who live beneath its canopies. This, in my mind, is the flimsy and unstable undercarriage which is never fixed. This is the zone where reckless presumption generates personal devastation and spiritual misdirection. And this is what marks us with perpetual immaturity, even as we imagine ourselves to be above all others in spiritual clarity.

The chapters that follow are articles—essays, in fact, on subjects pertaining to this area of concern. They are conversational, sometimes personal, intentionally non-technical; the pointed criticisms are pastoral in intent, being framed with a concern for ordinary people. I wanted them to be readable, interesting, and enlightening to the average reader. And I wanted to flag a few of those readers to stop and think for themselves.

The reader quite removed from this piece of the Christian pie, perplexed by Pentecostal and Charismatic types, and wondering what is with these people, may find some answers. The parroted Pentecostal-Charismatic response, of course, is "The Spirit." I would suggest, "The Spirit, yes, but sometimes lesser spirits of a malevolent sort, and many distinctly human drivers too." Not everything blowing here is the wind of the Holy Spirit.

Introduction

The Exhilaration and the Exasperation
. . . and the Holes in the Floor

I am Pentecostal. "Pentecostal to the bone," I say, and I have every intention of being one when I finish the course. I come by it honestly. Pentecostals were midwives to my conversion and framed my early Christian world. The Pentecostal Sub-Arctic Mission based in our town was the flagship of the national home missions department, and our local church was swollen with staffers who had come north to specifically work at the mission-managed hospital. Most of these, receiving accommodations and a stipend, rolled over their hospital salaries to fund the mission in its northern outreach. The commitment and zeal were striking, making our locale for many years something of a spiritual hot spot. Here Pentecostals, with some Evangelicals and a number who designated themselves "Charismatic," were engaged in a common cause and the climate was wonderfully open. I was imprinted early by the Charismatics who were typically the spiritual brighteners and initiators, and was warmly disposed toward them.

By the time my Bible college experience began, Pentecostals were generally middle class and had already moved uptown from across the tracks. Pentecostal Bible colleges were working toward accreditation with Evangelical agencies. Organizations like the Assemblies of God were distancing themselves from the Fundamentalists and actively courting the National Association of Evangelicals. The face of Bible colleges was changing with younger Pentecostals going out to obtain their seminary degrees and returning to occupy the teaching positions. The old guard was being shuffled to the sidelines, and tensions between the old Pentecostal way and the new directions were evident everywhere.

I recall this time of Pentecostal transition being attended with widespread disinterest and thinly veiled contempt for the Charismatic movement. Mainstream Pentecostals were scrambling for acceptance and a new face in a larger Christian world. They were, for the most part, looking for an Evangelical identity, not a Charismatic one, and wanting to distance themselves from the embarrassing Pentecostal fringe. Much of what was emerging in the Charismatic movement, I suspect, bore too much resemblance to their country cousins, from whom they were actively disassociating themselves. And they were not going back to that.

I too had reasons to be wary of the independents on the fringe and weary of some of the old guard within the denomination. I liked much of old Pentecostal preaching, even some of the thematic and analogical sermons loosely derived from Bible passages. But without a decent theological backdrop and overarching biblical frame of reference, this often went off the rails, and private agendas could take a teaching anywhere.

But I was never dismissive of Charismatics in general and many others were of the same mind. Many, suspicious of changes in the Pentecostal mainstream and recognizing a great moving of the Spirit, found new horizons and opportunities in the dynamic Charismatic movement. This great spiritual swell was, to me, God-driven both in its basic impulse and its incredible breadth. I also knew many Charismatics whom I liked and esteemed.

For many years, local Pentecostal churches enjoyed the benefits of having resident Charismatics, but these were invariably minorities in the congregations. Over time, the growing Evangelical component brought to many churches a quiet suppression of most things Charismatic and gave birth to a curious hybrid, the patently "un-Pentecostal" Pentecostal. Charismatics still struck me as the "brighteners," and against the backdrop of mainline Pentecostals in general, I intentionally identified myself as Pentecostal-Charismatic. (As earlier mentioned, I use the term "Pentecostal-Charismatic" in this sense consistently in the subsequent chapters—the "Pentecostal" part not referring to all who call themselves Pentecostal, but to those who share real common ground and interest, and readily mix with Charismatic believers). So when I was presented with an opportunity to teach at a Charismatic Bible school, I was ready for the new direction.

During these few years, the Charismatic renewal in the Okanagan Valley region crested, then gave way to an inevitable and necessary settling of accounts. Issues deferred and set aside in the heat of spiritual renewal rose up to meet us all on the journey back to ground level. Incompatible camps consolidated even as they coexisted under shared roofs, and this gave way to open competition to win people's hearts and minds. On a grander scale, major Charismatic church organizations and networks recruited from the general pool, and celebrated gurus accumulated clouds of devotees.

Doctrinal claims were often extreme, sometimes bizarre, and as the campaigning intensified, so did the confusion among those ill-equipped to process what was coming at them. A desperate need for order and organization had surfaced years earlier, but some of the discipleship and governance models implemented to preserve the results of the renewal were now criticized as authoritarian and spiritually abusive. Our independent Charismatic Bible school intentionally exposed students to the larger Pentecostal-Charismatic constituency through daily guest speaker slots. We found it increasingly necessary to side-step certain speakers and occasionally debrief our students. The open and tolerant Bible school model became difficult to maintain.

But there was much more going on than simply aspiring ministries clamoring for jurisdiction and prestige. Charismatics, pressed into defining themselves and their convictions, gathered into diverse but functioning church groups and dispersed in different directions. On a large scale, Pentecostal-Charismatic churches and networks evolved into insular societies. Bible schooling and ministry training had for some time moved in brand-specific directions. Even independent churches became all things to themselves, grooming their own people and growing their own leadership. Identifiable groups fenced themselves in, not just from a larger Christian world, but from other Pentecostal-Charismatics as well. Amid the turmoil of the times the hand of God was not easily discerned. Without fully realizing it, I too was caught up in the dispersion. But at the time I was exhausted and just wanted to get off the train.

New horizons opened for my wife and me to pursue further education, and we seized the opportunity. This permitted me to step back into the Pentecostal mainstream and simultaneously immerse myself in a program at a Christian and Missionary Alliance seminary. There was at that school a climate of openness and some affinity toward Pentecostals and Third Wave Evangelicals. Christian discipleship and spirituality were emphasized, and one professor was a visiting Anglican clergyman and identifiably Charismatic. I held much regard for those inside the CMA and benefited greatly from the education I received. But when faced with the idea of transitioning into the denomination, I knew I would never make the doctrinal accommodations. A later ministry-friendship with the Vineyard Fellowship came to a similar impasse. I am grateful for these ventures with other Christian groups, but I knew God would never let me camp with them. I was returning to the world I had hoped to escape, but by then I had the clarity to know I had been made for precisely that milieu. That was a decisive turn, and for many years now, my wife and I have been a few steps removed from the mainline Pentecostal churches and proximate to Charismatic people. This field has given us, together with our most exhilarating and exasperating moments, our most fruitful opportunities for ministry.

Still, that general Pentecostal-Charismatic pond is cluttered, and around its edges, contaminated. Charismatic types remain for me the "brighteners" in the Kingdom of God, the most natural first-responders to the Spirit of God. But as a movement we are both colorful and conflicted. We are competent in evangelism and have intimate familiarity with matters of the Spirit because we make large investments in those domains. Because possibilities in God are limitless, we presume there are no limitations on ourselves and endure a rugged learning curve because of that. We are too Laodicean to believe we may at the same time be theologically inept, biblically impoverished, and poorly taught. This happy naivety keeps us recycling our greatest mistakes. Pentecostal-Charismatics present a fierce edge for the Kingdom of God and hold forth the promise of endless possibilities in God, but we also spawn more hollow fads, tangents, major and minor heresies, and more Christian cults than any corner of Christ's church. The pond has real hazards, and long-standing levels of contamination show little sign of abating. Some quarters are rife with error precisely because they are perennially ripe for it. Yet we maintain a reluctance—if not an inability—to look at ourselves with eyes wide open.

I am not dismissing a movement in which I have invested a good part of my life. I can summarize my complaints in terms of three grave deficiencies. I would describe these as besetting sins which we superficially address and to which we are much inoculated. These too, like speaking in tongues and exuberant praise, have also become defining markers of Pentecostal-Charismatic culture:

- The first is our consuming spiritual pride and our settled conviction of unparalleled intimacy with God. This we play off against every faction on the horizon, ascribing more power and authority, more revelation knowledge, and more divine favor to ourselves than the lesser Pentecostals and Charismatics beyond our walls.

• The second is our propensity to play loosely with purported revelations, stamping our personal agendas and viewpoints with heavenly credentials, and using a "new thing" God is doing to entice recruits to our camp.

• The third is our refusal to functionally make the Bible our true baseline for belief and practice. We are desperately wanting for a biblical bottom line.

These have become identifiable cultural traits, pervasive because they are modelled in leadership as well as the rank and file, and perpetuated from one generation to the next. Offensive to onlookers, these are standard fare to cultural insiders. Each of these works with the other to nurture a predilection for preposterous claims: boastful assertions about ourselves, our ministries, and our experiences in God, inflated claims of authoritative revelations from God, and an eclectic *modus operandi* of convenience in our handling of Scripture. Each of these feeds the inherent dishonesty from which we generate endless spiritual spin about ourselves, our personal ministries and proximity to God, and our claims to inspired theological interpretation.

The chapters which follow address these three general grievances. They also underscore the believer's personal responsibility for their own life and personal jurisdiction over their own mind. One component of our freedom in Christ is the freedom and necessity to think for ourselves. Anyone led to believe they can do otherwise and do well in the Pentecostal-Charismatic world is definitely playing in the wrong field.

Long ago I read a statement in Edward O'Connor's widely read book, *The Pentecostal Movement in the Catholic Church* [1971] and immediately copied it on the inside cover of my Bible. I was overtaken by the picture of my own Pentecostal world and the truth it told about us:

> The Pentecostal Movement, even though it seems to be the work of the Holy Spirit in its root and principal impulse, is also a complex melange of human energies that in part correspond to the Spirit's plans but in part deviate from it, conflict with it, and counterfeit it.

Some forty years later, O'Connor's statement, I believe, is even more telling of the contemporary Pentecostal-Charismatic movement.

Chapter One

Spinning Doctrine in a
Pentecostal-Charismatic Milieu:
Running with a Revelation

As a young Bible college student, I often participated in weekend ministry teams, and one of these ventures took me to a small rural church. An elderly gentleman who was obviously the esteemed Bible teacher in this small congregation (a status he visibly enjoyed) disclosed that God had awakened him the previous night with a message. He said the Lord told him expressly that Joshua's famous declaration, "As for me and my house, we will serve the LORD," (Joshua 24:15, KJV) was not speaking of Joshua and his family or clan, but only of Joshua's personal resolution to follow God. "House," he said, was simply a reference to Joshua's physical body, and this was confirmed by 2 Corinthians 5:1 (KJV), which refers to our body as a "house." Therefore Joshua was speaking for himself only. I do not recall a point in his mini-lesson, except that the spiritual elder was once more affirmed in his role and the regulars went away happy to be blessed with such a good Bible teacher.

I remember my amusement at this curious juxtaposition of an authoritative personal revelation from God and one giant deductive leap to link two detached passages. I had seen this before, but this homey little Bible lesson captures in a snapshot some classic grassroots methodology, carried forward for decades by zealous Pentecostals and easily imported into the fledging and amorphous Charismatic movement where it has flourished. One makes a revelatory claim and sifts through the Bible assembling a rationale for it. This modus operandi is prolific throughout the Pentecostal-Charismatic milieu from top to bottom. It is the hermeneutic of the professing apostle and prophet, and also that of the ordinary person who has it continually modelled for him by speakers, pastors and popular Charismatic writers. Getting it from God, feeding it through the Bible, and running with the revelation. It is not amusing anymore.

Some Christians have too much vested interest to bother with good theological foundations. Aspiring gurus immediately discover this open-at-both-ends mode of framing beliefs—if applied cleverly and air-brushed with sophistication and spiritual authority—gives far more personal prestige and leverage than a simple Bible-based authority ever could. So it is doubtful the gaming with theology will ever be abated. Charismatic believers, however, should note that trumping objections with purported revelations and self-proclaimed spiritual authority, and superimposing authoritative interpretations on biblical passages, is precisely the method of the historical Christian cults. It is essentially the same game played by the same rules.

Much Charismatic belief structure is tenuously stitched together to propel another "new thing" God is doing. Despite the constant buzz about the Bible, not everyone is insistent that the Scriptures embody God's final and completed New Covenant revelation. Many are persuaded there is ongoing divine revelation of a similar caliber mediated through present-day apostles and prophets who are laying additional foundations. What was cautiously advanced twenty years ago has become more emboldened and no longer represents a small fringe constituency. The import is this: the Bible alone is not the baseline for truth and doctrine for growing numbers of

Pentecostal-Charismatics. They do not look for clear and unequivocal biblical support for faith and practice the way other conservative believers do because their divinely appointed leaders also bring an authoritative Word of God to them.

This comes with striking implications. Elite circles of self-proclaimed prophets and apostles progressively establish themselves beyond the scrutiny of anyone but themselves. They are accountable to no one but their associates, and ascribe to themselves a personal spiritual authority over those under their jurisdiction. These personalities are in some sense mini-popes and vaguely reminiscent of the traditional Roman Church where the Pope speaking *ex cathedra* ("from the chair") declares the words of Christ to his church. The magisterium gives the final word of interpretation to Scripture and church doctrine, and the priests function as essential spiritual mediators between Christ and his people.

I stated in my introduction that I was solidly Pentecostal. I am just as much Protestant to the core. I fully subscribe to the basic Reformation principles that the Scriptures alone are the inspired Word of God, that they alone are the final word on matters of faith and doctrine, and that they belong in the hands (and minds) of the people. I also endorse the priesthood of all believers. The believer does not need someone in authority to *mediate* his salvation or his ongoing spiritual growth and development in Christ, because Jesus himself fully and completely does that for him.

There were real causes underlying the Protestant Reformation, and as spiritual hierarchical structures rise to new heights in many parts of the Pentecostal-Charismatic world, so should our concerns about them. Is this a new revelation driven by God's Spirit to restore divine governance to Christ's church—or is it just a return of the wizard of Oz? Protestant reformers of all stripes correctly discerned what lay behind the curtains of ecclesiastical authority in their day. Beyond the spiritual airs, the mystique, the veils and the intimidating voice of God, they saw human hands pulling the levers and pressing the buttons—and fooling the people. So what's being played out before us?

Not everything Christian groups believe and practice can be dismissed as *incompatible* with Scripture simply because they are not spelled out for us in the Bible. Yet we must continually distinguish between what is biblically founded (and to what degree) and what is our embellishment or adaptation to times and places. Numerous matters are informed by biblical principles and examples, but the particulars and the directions—hopefully informed by God's Spirit as we seek him—are still worked out on the ground.

There is in the larger Christian world a broad consensus that church governance is neither finely tuned nor prescribed in detail in our New Testament books. It is consistently pointed out that instruction on leadership is more focused on character qualities and integrity than detailed functions of office. Evangelical camps disputing over church structure know the authority and legitimacy of their positions rest on the strength of their biblical arguments alone, and most would probably live with the stalemate. But most Pentecostal-Charismatics would never let their theological paradigms and church structures be placed on the same spiritual level as those of other Christian churches. The interpretative mold casts these things as directly ordained of God or biblical right down to the particulars, that the belief systems in their entirety have been barely tainted by human hands. In some circles, the issue could be closed with revelatory fiats that end all dispute—and end all sensible discussion too.

To be convincing, some beliefs must be made more "biblical" than they really are. We do this by imposing shapes and interpretations on individual passages of Scripture to conform them to our viewpoints. Definite shades of meaning are ascribed to specific Bible texts, then networked together with detailed arguments. The overall harmony and logical consistency of the final product is paramount, for this sells the package and masks our biased reasoning and skewed approach to Scripture.

To launch a new direction, one would need a huddle of trusting followers and have to drill them constantly, systematically and repeatedly casting our special light on an array of passages every time we refer to them. We would wisely minimize the opportunity for reflection and evaluation until our hearers themselves are well conditioned and instinctively associate our beliefs with crucial Bible passages. In due course, any reference to a key passage will trigger the meaning we have given it. If we do this broadly enough and cleverly enough with many Scripture passages, our adherents will begin to see for themselves that the complete doctrinal package is right there in the Scriptures and speaking to them. They may have their personal moment of "revelation" and take it as a Holy Spirit confirmation. And they might never know we have played with the Bible and played with their minds.

Only in the Pentecostal-Charismatic world, I am inclined to believe, can a collage of alleged God-showed-me's, authoritative declarations, appeals to one's office and authority, thinly-veiled warnings about missing this and missing God's will, personal values, proof texts, life experiences, tendentious interpretations and layers of deductions—only in this world can all that be sewn up in one large bundle, and peddled as though it was something lowered quite directly from heaven. Interpretive viewpoints and popular beliefs are consistently recast as "revelations" and bolstered to sell the idea that the full theological package is directed sourced from God. It is pitched as a divine disclosure, and therefore the "truth" and a direct expression of his will. This is spiritual scamming and fabrication in the least, akin to the "cunning craftiness" and "deceitful scheming" the apostle Paul speaks of in Ephesians 4:14. What would never fly in a larger Christian world is a staple to Charismatic culture and countless numbers consume it every day.

How does this happen? Pentecostal-Charismatics add several components to the mix, things common to their religious culture, that make them vulnerable. Mindless trust, ongoing psychological conditioning, virtual autonomy at the highest levels of leadership, comparative isolation from a larger Christian world, endless layers of spiritual spin, and faulty assumptions about the Bible are key examples. Beliefs can be mere assertions without credible evidence in their own right. This occurs in any religious world but jumps up several notches in the Pentecostal-Charismatic milieu. This is a zone where numerous individuals claim high callings in God. Believing multitudes see such persons in a special place between themselves and God, and are much disposed toward them. Here even bare-faced assertions may be super-charged. The raw power of bald assertion has always been a dynamic force in the classical Pentecostal orb. But in contemporary Charismatic domains, empty declarations are easily imbued with the aura of divine authority.

If one consistently immersed their mind in reading the Scriptures as they present themselves, they might never come to the conclusions other parties are making and never embrace the claims they are imposing on their lives. Pentecostals and Charismatics in general are not great students of Scripture, and typically inclined to engross themselves in popular books and DVDs. Here they are led along trails someone else has carved through the Bible, adding one thing to another and enticing them to embrace viewpoints and beliefs they could never critically evaluate. John Wesley, I believe, counselled an opposite approach—reading the Bible deeply and reading other books widely.

Much Pentecostal-Charismatic belief is not based so much on clear statements of Scripture but on the *consistency of the arguments* that bind them together. Numerous conclusions would never come to mind in a normal reading of the books of the Bible. They have artificially been imposed upon the Bible, slipped in from the side-lines by smooth arguments that accommodate the assumptions of the human interpreter. Whenever we have a belief system or a theology built upon one inference after another we do not have much.

Those of us in the Pentecostal-Charismatic milieu should immediately take pause whenever we start believing our sub-group or package is a precise expression of God's will and truth. We should tell ourselves we are fooling ourselves whenever we think our shared convictions and interpretations are themselves the "truth." We spot the error when Mormons and Jehovah's Witnesses lay claim to divinely inspired theology, but are surprisingly accommodating and blind in one eye to subtle claims of the same in our own circles.

The Bible alone is the inspired Word of God. Our interpretations are not. When we cast our theological paradigms and church models in the language of *revelation, deeper truth,* or *present truth,* we're playing the classic Pentecostal "God-showed-me" card. We are claiming spiritual authority and special graces for hearing God's voice and understanding the Scriptures that ordinary Christian people do not have and cannot access. We are replaying old church dogma and imitating familiar cultic ploys, and setting the stage for indoctrination instead of authentic Christian education. Implicit is the conviction that this is God-breathed truth for our times. The insinuation is clear that this—because it comes from God—stands beyond normal scrutiny and evaluation.

Recent decades have seen the rise and demise of several deeper truth movements, each purporting to have been more anointed, more enlightened, and more obedient that the last one. The initial aspiration to transcend denominational barriers, escape the plight of sleepy churches, and speak to believers everywhere typically turned a corner. Soon enough, they were circling their wagons, insulating themselves from other believers and outside influences, and becoming more sectarian than the church structures they were reacting against. Each had grossly overstated its role in bringing restoration and reformation to Christ's church and history quickly recast them in a much dimmer light than they had placed themselves. Not to worry, though! In the larger Pentecostal-Charismatic world, new gurus and new groupies are continually rising up to run with a revelation and repeat the cycle. Old goods are repackaged, a new spiritual spin is added, and what's gone around keeps coming around again!

Chapter Two

Polishing the Spiritual Persona:
Pride in a Sunday Suit

Our most besetting sin—closest to the surface and always oozing through—is our spiritual pride. We are smug. Proximity to spiritual power encounters and God's workings, together with our personal spiritual experiences and giftings, make us heady. These things in combination with our unrelenting conviction that the most ordinary person can and does hear from God, and our general sense of intimacy with him, bait us to think loftily of ourselves. Our church cultures too, because we have created them, embody and institutionalize our collective pride. Every Christian sub-culture has its gauges for informally determining and dispensing spiritual status. Our world is no exception, and our ever-aspiring self learns to play to these things.

Spiritual Pride in the Personal Journey

Puffed-up DNA is deeply woven into the Pentecostal-Charismatic fabric and few escape its imprint on our hearts. We know, of course, that Jesus fully accepts us the way we are. But at ground level where we work it out, the combination of spiritual strength, confidence and a victorious Christian life is the litmus test, the unwritten standard to which we measure ourselves. We also learn to read others to see where they are in relation to ourselves. Within moments of an introduction, we intuitively know if someone is projecting themselves above us or beneath us on the spiritual plane, or opening themselves as an equal in Christ. This little posturing game is common occurrence, and many of us are attuned and know it well. Pentecostalized pride is in our bones, so much so that thinly-veiled pride is a normal for us; because of that, we have remarkable tolerance for high levels of spiritual strutting in others.

Conversion to Christ infused me with spiritual life and wonderfully introduced me to my heavenly Father. At the same time it thrust me into a Pentecostalized view of the world. I had to learn to swim in a river that was both dynamically alive and prone to turbulence. I would not trade the journey. I consider my heritage to be rich, in large part because its Christian culture was evangelistic and generally "zealous of spiritual gifts" (1 Corinthians 14:12, KJV). Yet beneath the surface it created its own climate of pressure to measure up, and correspondingly the warm glow of pride when one felt successful and sudden deflation when one did not. This context cradled much unholy ambition, though this was not easily discerned, obscured as it was by a bigger picture of doing God's work and a busy Christian life.

When we are young in the Lord or insecure, God's activity in our life becomes desirable for a couple of reasons. It gives us "face" in the presence of our peers and permits us, for the moment at least, to believe there is something genuinely spiritual about our life too. The unspoken wish is not only for God to act mightily, but for us to be present and visible to others when he does. Our prayer to God to use us is easily stuffed with a mixed agenda. The journey of finding ourselves in God and growing into our gifts—which should naturally unfold in the processes of life— is made unnecessarily arduous and confusing. Charismatic clamor draws too much attention to itself, and triumphalism alone stirs our courage and ambition, but gives us no direction for life. These become distractions, trumping gentler voices who counsel patience, simplicity and an inner journey. They also mute the quiet, persistent voice of God's Spirit. Humility and patience are not benchmarks of Pentecostal-Charismatic culture. We look for short-cuts and divinely dramatic quick fixes, and personal spiritual clarity can be a long time coming.

Our Fascination with the Great Man of God

The perennial temptation is to look large, larger than we really are, in the eyes of our brothers and sisters. The larger spiritual arena puts a premium on zeal, victory, and spiritual power, talking the talk and presenting oneself as strong, well-hinged, and successful in the personal journey. Expectations run high among zealots and always beget a class of larger-than-life, living heroes. They themselves, and not merely their books and messages, embody the aspirations of ordinary people. Today it is the Charismatic celebrity and prominent apostle or prophet who has updated and upstaged the traditional Pentecostal evangelist/revivalist, the classic man-of-the-hour whose gifted anointing and intimacy with God were shrouded in mystery. That mystique was cultivated and still is to some extent, but with more subtlety. God's special servants, in the Pentecostal-Charismatic sphere, are not merely highly respected ministers and authors; they are icons with large numbers of deeply loyal followers who personally identify with them and hang on their every word. The great person of God makes them feel secure and strong—and proud. This syndrome, and the grand scale of it, is to me unhealthy at the least and quasi-idolatrous at the extreme, a picture of misplaced attachment and vulnerability. Yet no one speaks of it as spiritual displacement, an idolatry of the heart or an impingement on one's faithfulness to Jesus Christ. Anyone so given over to mere human personalities is meat hanging on the rack to the predatory opportunist. And those at the center of the attention can choose to play with that, or not.

Primping Ourselves for Public Consumption

Personal insecurities and pride, coupled with socio-spiritual pressures, entice us to grow personas, public images of ourselves to mask our weaknesses and project our strengths. They are not an authentic us. We are selling a version of ourselves in a public market and we are engaged in the serious game of Pentecostal one-upmanship. Interesting to me is how believers from Anabaptist roots—Mennonites, Hutterites, and the Amish—have consistently differentiated themselves and broken ranks over questions of "Who is least tainted by the world around us?" Classical Pentecostals had a shorter but intense run with strict "holiness" religion and the "clothesline" gospel, but that had dissipated by my time. Today Pentecostal-Charismatic one-upmanship always revolves around the unspoken questions of "Who is most spiritual, that is, most full of the Holy Spirit and most proximate to the presence of God among us?" and "Who has more spiritual authority?"

We find ways to testify of what God has done, and give him glory for it (or so it seems) and assert our significance too. There are ways to engage in friendly conversation and insinuate our spiritual rank at the same time. There are ways to accrue personal status to ourselves when the Spirit of God is moving in striking ways, like hustling over to the hot spot and inserting ourselves into the action with visible displays and prophetic-sounding declarations. Yes, we have our ways to be seen and noticed.

Attention-seeking behaviors are not relegated to the young and the immature. Overreaching ambition is on full display across the Pentecostal-Charismatic spectrum in an endless scramble for recognition, prestige, and authority. Self-seeking leaders spin the notion that they live and breathe in a realm quite removed from ordinary believers. Teaching ministries had the main stage in the '60s and '70s, and prophetic ministries stepped to the forefront and established their profiles in the '80s and '90s. Today apostleship is the pinnacle of everything. Popular personalities have moved onwards and upwards into purportedly higher offices as the decades have passed, continuously keeping themselves current and in the limelight wherever it has swung. Authentic apostolic ministries, I believe, are those engaged in undertakings of great scope, planting churches and enabling pastors, overseeing the general work of God's Kingdom—and too busy and too personally disinterested to flaunt themselves and their callings. Suspect to me are all those who preach themselves more than they preach Christ, solicit personal spiritual commitments to themselves, and lift their personal statuses to ever-increasing heights on the authority pyramid.

The clamber among Pentecostal-Charismatics for letters behind our names and the parade of fivefold ministry titles are in large measure persona-building strategies, and sometimes blatantly so. Within the Charismatic world, even a thinly academic degree delivers considerable status and disproportionate personal mileage. The letters often suggest an educational experience and exposure that runs far deeper than it does. Any investment in training and education is significant and commendable, but higher degrees insinuate a standard. They presume a depth of research and breadth of learning that an additional year at the same school and a major research paper do not deliver. I am no fan of stuffy accreditation standards, but on this one the pretentious airs are cultivated on both sides of the fence.

A pastor of an average-sized congregation can attend a conference on apostolic leadership and be surprised to meet "apostles" pastoring churches with significantly smaller congregations. Can this be anything more than persons aspiring to be something they are not? Similarly, one may consider God is calling and leading them into pastoral ministry, yet they are not a "pastor" in anyone else's eyes, nor should they expect to be, until they are doing the

actual work of pastoring a circle of believers. A student once introduced himself to me as an "end-time prophet." I don't know about
the end-time bit, but he was certainly giving me an omen of things
to come in the classroom. Striving and reaching! Like Diotrephes,
we love the pre-eminence (3 John 9). We love to be first, and we
keep devising ways to project ourselves beyond measure.

Spiritual Pride and Spiritual Error

Pride is the underground stream that fuels a deception of ourselves,
derailing us from the simplicity of following Jesus and carrying us
into doctrinal confusion and distraction. Pride is prerequisite to
error, and error is always attended by prideful elitism. They are
close cousins. But even prideful personal claims must be driven
through the Scriptures, even superficially, because this is how new
teachings are invested with the Bible's air of authority and transformed into God's program. And being God's thing gives leaders
the leverage to press their own oversight and claims on those gathered around them. In a Pentecostal-Charismatic domain, whenever
home-spun theological methods prevail, collective pride invariably
gets embedded in the belief system itself. Often the group sees
itself in biblical typology and assigns itself the great task of restoring truth to Christ's church.

Errant systems never make it easy to leave, though it is comparatively easy to sign up, like the familiar check valve which flips up
to permit one-directional flow, but flips down immediately when
the flow is reversed. Pride is one of several elements hindering
one's exit. It is especially difficult to face the role our pride and
spiritual ambition played in our being taken captive. We reached
for the bait. We wanted to believe God was specifically calling us
to link arms with his special corps of anointed servants. We were
willing to trade off much of our personal freedom in Christ because
we wanted to believe this new thing could fast-track us to a higher

spirituality and afford us closer proximity to God than Christ alone could give us. We were seduced by clever people, but we were also seduced by our own prideful impulses. And both the errant teaching and the perpetrators sanctioned our pride. They encouraged us to nurture an exalted sense of ourselves—as long as we kept our place and followed the script.

Closing Note

We can be too ambitious and grasping, and never content. Yet because it is all conducted under the banner of ministry to the Lord and service to his people, we pass it all off as good. When we have too much to prove, too much to lose, and too much to gain, we can never be our ordinary yet authentic selves in Christ.

Pentecostal and Charismatic spirituality has never been particularly introspective. In our world, pride is rarely honestly addressed until it reaches outlandish proportions, or someone hits a brick wall, but even then, the enduring lessons are never widely appropriated. We are conditioned to be active and involved, not contemplative and reflective. Consequently, we are not attuned to the grave contradictions both in our own hearts and in the larger Charismatic culture. How do we keep making ourselves look large in our own eyes and other people's minds, and at the same time *decrease*, that is, become diminished—so that Christ can *increase* and have pre-eminence? "He must become greater, I must become less" (John 3:30).

This is our enigma. Polishing our image and strutting our spiritual stuff is as perennially Pentecostal as speaking in tongues. But it contradicts what we are called to be. And it is quite a trick to convince others we can be filled with the Holy Spirit and full of ourselves at the same time.

Chapter Three

Shoehorning the Bible to Fit Our Beliefs: Looking through Colored Lenses

Feeling strongly about something does not make it true. But when we *feel* something is true, nothing will easily convince us otherwise! And this pervasive human trait crawls right into our study of the Bible. When something resonates with us, we are hooked, and even a careful examination of Scripture will not easily pry us away. One line from the movie *The Sentinel* (2006) captures it all: "Once you have a gut feeling, the only evidence you will hear is that which reinforces your gut feeling." How true!

"Spiritualized" Interpretation—I'd Love It Except I Hate It!

I enjoyed some of the old typological sermons that walked the listener through a lengthy Old Testament story, shaving off correspondences and lessons for the Christian journey at numerous points in the message. I loved the creative literary art and delighted in the two stories being told at the same time. I was captivated and inspired by the combination of words and pictures. This was once common fare in evangelical preaching, but I was part of a generation that reacted wholesale to this mode of interpretation. Our messages were expository, closer to the biblical text, and often less interesting. We had to accommodate the looser, analogical approaches of the New Testament writers in their handling of certain Old Testament passages, and how they artfully played with particular correspondences. Furthermore, the apostle Paul tells us the Israelite experience in their wilderness sojourns are "examples to keep us from setting our hearts on evil things as they did" (1 Corinthians 10:6). Obviously God intended that we should see ourselves in those stories, and that gave us pause too.

But we had a point and still do. Analogies we create from Scripture passages can go anywhere we want to take them. Unless specifically given to us in certain passages or alluded to by biblical writers, we are the ones who deduce the correspondences and weave them back through the biblical text. They are not in the Bible as some kind of mystical layer above the literal words; they are in our minds. What we are doing is making a *practical application*, not uncovering a hidden spiritual meaning. In fact, this occurs whenever we draw lessons from historical Bible stories. We are seeing parallels between ourselves and them, and transferring the spiritual insights to our own circumstances.

A memorable sermon in the early years of the Latter Rain-mainline Pentecostal schism was *Running Without a Message*, a spiritualized take on the two messengers bringing David news of his son Absalom. The Latter Rainers were the Cushite who brought an accurate account of the events (i.e., the great move of God's Spirit) and the Pentecostal mainliners were the bumbling Ahimaaz who saw the great commotion but did not know what it was. This was classic Pentecostal one-upmanship at its best, artfully creative and delivered with one masterstroke—and biblical to boot! This example underscores how, with spiritualizing exegesis, we can make it *mean* whatever we choose—and if we choose, we can really make it *mean*.

Spiritualized interpretation is always an imposition upon the biblical text of what we already believe and assume. In the hands of a mature believer with a broad biblical foundation, it may be inspiring. But for establishing biblical foundations, formulating theology, articulating our most basic beliefs, and defining our distinctives, it is disastrous. It is, at this level, "junk." It blatantly inserts human agendas and personal notions into a process that should impose the strictest discipline on our biases and represent our best attempt to determine what God is saying to us in his Word. To bring a full bottle of personal biases to the table to open the discussion makes the whole business pretentious.

My favorite among all my sermons is a spiritualized message, and I have few of them. It comprises a literal storytelling of Paul's horrific sea voyage in Acts 27, complete with historical backgrounds and cultural trimmings. But alongside the literal story, I laid another sound track, an unfolding picture of the great spiritual storm, the trial of incredible proportions, and the one true God who alone can rescue us. It is not original; I heard a pastor do this once and knew I could paint a spiritual-journey picture of my own.

On one occasion when I preached this message, an older gentleman spoke to me afterwards saying God would continue to reveal to me the deeper meanings in this chapter. His words suggested I had peeled some layers off the onion but still had some distance to go. Layers of spiritual meaning above the literal? Not really. I had taken personal liberties and creatively played with the story. I shaped and nuanced the analogy. I might believe God gave me the inspiration to do so but no one should believe that on my say so. And I filled that analogy with good stuff, the standard components from centuries of Christian spiritual journeying and sound counsel for walking through deep trials. But none of that was the *meaning*. It was at its core a creative *application* of life principles already understood and widely accepted in Christian circles.

Our Deductive Logic Can Snow Us—and Others Too

I suspect most Charismatically-inclined people assume the Bible is their final word and judge in matters of faith and practice. But at ground level, a lot of popular teaching and theology is never measured against the Bible with real discipline and diligence. Many are more attuned to what their leaders and popularizers are saying to them than anything God is saying to them in the Scriptures. In our world, the Bible is easily *voiced over* by:

1. appeals to "revelations" to fill gaps where Scripture is silent, obscure, or non-supportive of what is claimed,
2. simple fiats and pronouncements by self-professed spiritual authorities,
3. prescriptions and particulars exceeding what is written and what is clearly taught, and
4. strings of deductive reasoning gathering passages into tidy, appealing packages.

These end-runs around a responsible and accountable handling of Scripture are prevalent in Pentecostal-Charismatic circles. Well into a second generation now, former points of reference have faded off the horizon, leaving entire communities so fully conditioned to this modus operandi they cannot discern how flawed and reckless it is.

Deductive logic—that is, starting with a general premise or assumption and sifting through the Bible for proofs to build our case—can fool us! A well-crafted argument can be convincing even when the evidence is weak. The logical consistency hooks us and reinforces conclusions that initially seem valid and true. We can blindly run down rails someone else has laid out and fail to weigh the evidence for ourselves at each point along the track. But biblical truth must rest on what Bible passages actually teach or clearly infer, not the rational case used to link one passage to another. A brick wall held together by particularly thick seams of mortar is second rate and structurally unsound. In general, the biblical evidence—with due regard for grammar, context and historical backgrounds—must be allowed to do most of the speaking for itself, and do so on its terms.

The wife of a former professor, who was passionate and articulate on his pet issues, often told him the way he argued his case made it sound much stronger than it actually was, as if contrary views had no leg to stand on. She was right, and this happens a lot. A big investment in presentation and framing cannot carry the argument without good biblical evidence with real weight.

The more rationalization and explanation needed to bridge the gaps and make the case, the more likely we are driving our own theme into the Bible, and not truly finding it there. Good inductive evidence, from specific passages, is vital at every link in the chain. But objective Bible study is impossible when we have our own agenda, when we are already convinced of something and determined to prove it. We Pentecostal-Charismatics are vulnerable because our personal spiritual experiences easily become our starting points for our beliefs and assumptions. This is *a priori* reasoning, starting with a private conviction and then proving it is true. In defense of the Pentecostal-Charismatic, it is equally true that the Evangelical's lack of particular spiritual experiences has also given him a special set of eyeglasses. His "experience" has shaped his theology too, and he casts anything in Scripture of a Pentecostal flavor into his own boxes. Still true is the fact that intense spiritual experiences pack a deep imprint. These, on a practical level, may seem to be more direct *words* from God than statements in Scripture. We home-grow our own habits of jumping to conclusions without building biblical bridges to get us there. And the clichéd "This comes by revelation" is simply a spiritual smokescreen that conceals these big deductive leaps!

Our hasty generalizations run ahead of the biblical evidence and sound reasoning because we already know what we believe and are essentially combing the Bible for "proofs" to piggy-back on its authority and endorsement. And when we encounter statements suggesting something other than what we are looking for, we gloss over texts or mute them to dovetail with our views. We all possess a natural reluctance to truly consider evidence that softens our case, and we can quickly upgrade that to a stubborn refusal. Our biases have deep emotional attachments and vested interests, and they will not easily roll over and die.

This kind of shoehorning distorts God's word and God's intention, and gives rise to much bad theology for which Pentecostals and Charismatics are well-known. *Bad* not simply because of the flawed inferences and tendentious interpretations on which it is planted, but *bad* because in its application it impinges on personal spiritual freedom in Christ and sanctions the extension of religious authority beyond biblical parameters. We have a choice: we can stretch and force-fit our favorite glove over the hand, or we can look for the kind of glove that will most naturally fit the hand. Are we reading the Bible to find what it is saying to us, or are we reading the Bible with some specific use in mind? It is one thing to scrape together support for our views; it is quite another to honestly search for a biblical foundation.

We Can't See the Ground When We're Flying in the Fog

How is it so many people, who easily pick up the flow of thought and context in an operator's manual or a magazine article, find no need to strain the usual meaning of words or revamp the message until they pick up a Bible? Suddenly the normal use of language in the Bible is abandoned and the quest for mystical interpretations, cryptic messages, and special revelations takes over. These approaches have no objective limitations or discipline to restrain our private impulses and imaginations. There is no method in them that people could ever agree upon, just the belief that the spiritually enlightened person and the truly devoted heart can uncover hidden truths and perceive deeper meaning in Bible passages. Any interest such persons have in the divine disclosure God gave us in ordinary human language is marginal. Their fascination is with the secret things God has evidently concealed from plain view—and from spiritually average persons.

But there is no "deeper meaning" in a passage than the one the original human writer, under inspiration of the Holy Spirit, intended there to be. And if we are not making a sincere effort to get back to that, we are floating around in our ethereal inner space. *Meaning is not personally negotiable.* It is not something God withholds from everybody else and discloses to us. Still, thousands of Charismatics immerse themselves in some version of esoteric spiritual knowledge. They see themselves party to divine intuitive knowledge and walking in a dimension quite apart from lesser Pentecostal-Charismatics who, not having linked arms with them nor accepted their "truth," have been left outside. The spiritual differentiation between the Greek words *logos* and *rhema* was a contrivance, and evolved into a pretentious and faddish way of grading levels of spirituality. It is representative of the fluffy and fuzzy stuff used to spin spiritual beliefs, but has nothing to do with getting down to the real intent and meaning of Scripture.

Sometimes our reading of Scripture seems like old news and dull data-gathering; other times it is warmly illuminating. Some occasions are interrupted by heightened moments when God's Spirit bears witness to and directly personalizes specific verses and phrasing. Even creatively "free" adaptations that lift passages from their original context and enliven them to directly address matters in our lives are neither a rarity nor over-the-edge mysticism. But we might confuse Holy Spirit *applications* such as these with *meaning.* Living encounters with God's Spirit, deeply imprinting as they are, do not determine what a passage means. And the active mystical pursuit of these experiences from our end quickly goes to seed.

We ought not to think of the Word of God as a pliable medium through which the Holy Spirit keeps unfolding present truths and private messages to us. An endless stream of personalized guidance and direction suggests a questionable mysticism, a passive and mushy mind, or a pretentious game. The Bible is made less a rock to stand on than a gel-like medium channelling heavenly communications to us. We need to get beyond ourselves and get back to the plain meaning and intention of Scripture. Inspired by the Holy Spirit, the original manuscripts of the Bible are God's Word to us in ordinary human languages. Their words and phrases mean what they originally meant in those languages, and in particular, what the original writers understood and intended them to mean. At this level, the Scriptures are saying the same thing to all peoples everywhere. And this is the objective understanding and meaning of Scripture we need to be looking for when we study the Bible. I like Gordon Fee's summation: "It can never mean what it never meant." Making personal applications from the meaning is a necessary yet subsequent step.

Yes, God's Spirit may illuminate an obscure passage to us. Yet it remains for us to convince others through sound reasoning, historical and cultural backgrounds, and biblical language studies. When we resort to playing "revelation" cards to pitch our interpretations and give us extra leverage, we are cheating and undoubtedly misleading ourselves as well. In fact, we Pentecostal-Charismatics have fabricated a culture of cheating at exegesis and bullying our way forward with trumped-up authoritative claims and God-showed-me's. We default to these wild cards to make Scripture walk on all fours, and avoid the difficult tasks of honest biblical research and clear thinking.

But popular perceptions of knowing biblical truth get deeply embedded and never completely go away. Some are convinced they get it straight from God. Others are persuaded God channels a pure stream of truth to them through their spiritual leaders or church organization. And a cursory appeal 2 Corinthians 3:6—"the letter kills, but the Spirit gives life"—gives them a biblical exemption from any further explanation. One obvious question arises, however: When two purportedly Spirit-led authorities make contrary claims about something in the Bible, how do we break the deadlock? We must appeal to some biblical authority beyond each of their claims of having a personal hotline to God. As deflating as the process may seem to hyper-spiritual sensibilities, that means getting down to the plain and natural meanings of words and phrases of the passages in question. Plain old historical-grammatical Bible interpretation, and all the hard grinding that implies, is still the bottom line.

Sound Biblical Interpretation is Not a Best Seller

Given occasion to push whatever I thought would deeply benefit the most people in the Christian world in which I live and move, I would opt for something along the lines of sound and sensible Bible interpretation. My experience, of course, tells me I would find few takers in the Pentecostal-Charismatic milieu and would assuredly starve if I went on the road with this stuff. This, for most, would have no more appeal than eating chalk. Many think they are just too smart for it. I find that unfortunate because anyone who seriously invests themselves in this direction invariably finds new lenses for reading the Bible with clarity and consistency—and confidence. It would be with them forever, deepen their biblical footings, and richly enhance their ministry to others.

Hermeneutics is a word to choke on, but the concept is not. It essentially means to explain or interpret, and considers sensible guidelines to help us come to terms with the meaning of Scripture. It should not be a stuffy academic pursuit, but rather an attempt to bring in at ground level some enlightened common sense and responsibility to our handling of God's Word. Good interpretation directly challenges our obsessions with ourselves and what the Bible means to us, and moves us forward in a lifelong attempt to hear what the Bible is saying on its own terms—and what it is saying to all people.

"What it means to me" has been a launching pad for many strange beliefs and a lot of bad theology, which finds no end in Pentecostal-Charismatic domains, and no end in sight. Much is wonderful in this world of Spirit-filled believers, but biblically and doctrinally it bears much resemblance to the Wild West. One does not keep trekking successfully for long without picking up some travel smarts and some personal competence in reading and understanding the Bible for themselves. Many winds converge in this space and theological disturbance is a constant.

Chapter Four

What Does "Error" Look Like?
It Looks Like Truth, Even Better!

Error, in a religious context, refers to a deviation from an accepted standard of truth and doctrinal soundness. The term in general usage often implies a mistake, something unintentional and done in ignorance, but in this context it refers specifically to false teachings and false beliefs. And once these are fully flowered, one has to doubt if there ever was something unintentional about them.

What does a serious spiritual error look like? If it is finely crafted and well-managed, I would think it should look marvellously intriguing to the aspiring and diligent believer who wants more of God and desires to please him. Error is always elitist and its proponents, by virtue of the enlightenment they have received, score themselves a cut above the rest. "Specious" is the perfect descriptor, because well-packaged error typically has showy appeal yet something suspect about it. "Duplicity" is a good word too, because the full picture with all its implications is only slowly unrolled, and the trusting soul is seduced into its orb by increments.

Doctrinal and spiritual errors are deeper and carry more consequences than Christian fads and novelties. They are never honest mistakes for long. There is too much contrivance and manipulation in the systematizing process, and it is too cleverly formatted. A serious spiritual error is more aptly an enterprise, and as presented in the New Testament, a curious juxtaposition of seducing spirits and active human agents. It is propelled by contrivance and enticement. If there was some initial naivety it is quickly lost as shrewd strategies, pseudo-scholarship, and indoctrinating methodologies are added to get the program on the road. *Deceitful scheming* is the typical New Testament shade on it.

Redrawing the Lines Between "Us" and "Them"

Errant groups hastily redefine themselves against the larger Christian world around them, separating and distinguishing themselves from other believers whom they judge to be misled and spiritually impoverished. This differentiation is bold and dismissive, for they have become the true seekers of God, a faithful remnant that is more devoted, more enlightened, and more divinely empowered than all others. Yet the group still needs proximity to the larger pool of Pentecostal-Charismatic believers as this provides the opportunities for conversation and recruitment.

Duplicity and shape-shifting are inescapable because the necessity to appear much like other believers and nurture connections is in constant tension with a corresponding necessity to remain aloof and untouched by them. But whenever it is expedient, faithful devotees easily and instantly differentiate themselves. This shifting of colors is a predictable indicator that their deepest loyalties are elsewhere. Proponents of error play with two faces. Systematic error requires well-defined demarcations between those on the inside and those on the outside if it is to sell itself as God's timely answer for the church today. And the sect works hard to keep their defining elements constantly before the faces of their membership. Among Charismatics and Pentecostals, the wall is raised between those who walk in the new revelation and those who do not, between those who have accepted the "present truth" and those who have rejected it. This is always the bottom line!

Magnifying the Hierarchy Within

Systematic error grossly enlarges the roles and the authority of its human agents. Its man-made structures and leadership models are presented as divinely instituted and assigned disproportionate stakes in the administration of God's kingdom, Christ's church, and the personal lives of God's people. Authority levels are sharply defined with very specific roles.

In the Pentecostal-Charismatic sphere, the human mediation of God's gifts and graces presumes a larger role than the New Testament gives it. Human beings—by virtue of their offices—are made essential players in the distribution and impartation of spiritual gifts and ascribed exaggerated roles as personal spiritual "coverings" for the flock. They presume special and exalted roles for themselves in spiritual warfare against powers in high places and establish themselves as essential human mediators between God and those within their oversight. The consistent inference is that they, because of their divinely ordained authority, can bestow spiritual graces upon those in their spiritual jurisdictions, and by implication, can block them also. Leadership holds great personal power over those in their charge.

Human leadership is raised up several notches in any errant community, and insinuates itself deeply into the personal domains of its adherents. It presumes a life-management role that begets submissive dependence. The attention to jurisdiction and control is a constant in these circles, and so is the continual drumroll of justifying rationales.

Error raises the human component to new heights and stuffs it in places where the Bible does not. By recasting spiritual leadership as spiritual intermediaries, it quietly diminishes the unique claim and all-sufficient role of Jesus himself over the believer's inner sanctum and usurps several specific functions of the Holy Spirit. The outcome is predictable. No longer is it Jesus alone who mediates before the Father on behalf of the believer. The individual has been convinced by those above him that they are now standing between him and Jesus. That, I would say, is one big game-changer—and one blatant heresy!

Playing the Interpretative Pipeline to God

Every errant group claims a direct source in God for its beliefs and practices, and projects itself as the custodian of a pure stream of truth. The assertion is never simply that they are basing their beliefs as closely as possible on true biblical statements, but that their beliefs are in and of themselves the "truth." The Roman Catholic Church has traditionally held that accurate interpretation rests with the magisterium, the teaching authority of the church, and when the Pope speaks "from the chair" he is speaking in the stead of Christ, and it is the truth. The faithful Catholic has, for many decades now, been invited to *read* the Bible for himself, but unlike the Protestant tradition, he has never been invited to *interpret* it for himself. The distinction is important. Similarly, the "truth" for the Jehovah's Witness comes off the upper deck of the Watchtower Society, overseen by its highest directors. Individual adherents fully understand they are not capable of interpreting the Scriptures for themselves because the Holy Spirit ("God's active force" to them) only works through the visible organization, that is, the Society. And everyone understands that.

Charismatics are not always known for their attachments to church organizations per se, but many are distinguished by their deep personal loyalties to leaders. These loyalties often defer to leadership as essential recipients of truth and final interpreters on Scriptural questions. As in the Roman Catholic Church and the

Watchtower Society, here too authority on matters of interpretation comes to rest with the few at the top deemed to truly walk in revelation and speak for God.

Appeals to Bible passages and strained interpretations, personal convictions and hunches, claims of private revelations, and brazen declarations are woven together into belief systems. These are stamped as revelatory from God and peddled to the masses as God's present truth for the times. The assertion that this array of beliefs, this theology, is inspired of God—that it comes from him instead of human personalities—is the essential error which makes it a false teaching. As a general foundational platform of faith and practice for believers this is "slush," yet its appeal to Pentecostal-Charismatics is unwavering.

What Jesus Has Done—Plus Personal Spiritual Scores

Error needs spiritual leverage over its adherents. It needs control and a means to shift devotion to God toward its own ends, a carrot to dangle before the horse. Errant Christians neither appreciate nor respect the liberty that the individual believer has been given in Christ, and undertake their own interventions. Yet they can only be successful to the degree they can seduce others into a Jesus-Plus-Something-Else religion. As a young believer, I had a brief stint in a Pentecostal cult where spiritual salvation was not simply based on faith in Christ and a born-again experience—it was also conditional on a personal "oneness" revelation of Jesus himself as the Father, the Son, and the Holy Spirit, water baptism specifically in the name of Jesus, and Holy Spirit baptism with speaking in tongues. But even with that there was no consolation because of the endless list of holiness requirements and the burden of measuring up. Purporting to be the portal to life and the true knowledge of God, this errant system brought bondage and despair.

Most contemporary Charismatic error is savvy enough not to assault the fundamental doctrine of salvation through faith in Christ alone, but uses other avenues to exploit spiritual insecurities and insert themselves into Christian lives. One's basic eternal status may be secure, but what about their prospect of coming to their full maturity in Christ, having God's full favor, walking in revelation and victory, or being a truly Spirit-led believer in these last days? How can one have this if he dismisses the present truth God is revealing through modern-day apostles and prophets, and rejects their spiritual covering and direction? Yes, the believer has Jesus, but to attain God's ultimate intentions and enter deeper realms in God, one must embrace what the Holy Spirit is doing now and come into proper alignment to his delegated authorities. In short, the believer is assaulted with the dreadful prospect he has an impoverished future in God without them. That is the typical pitch thrown to the emotionally insecure but spiritually aspiring Pentecostal-Charismatic, and that is what entices (and frightens) them to buy into the Jesus-plus-something-else program.

Error is overly prescriptive, imposing new demands and expectations on the adherents. There is always the weight of legalism in any errant system, but that legalism may have diverse faces. It may be heavy-handed or gently manipulative, but compliance and conformity to the inner life of the group is never negotiable. The need to constantly measure up and perform as expected never goes away, because that is the culture and cohesive fabric of the group.

Grasping for a fast-track to spiritual power and esoteric knowledge, and a place for ourselves in God's inner-circle, brings only bitter fruit. We, like Eve, can be seduced and deceived. We can trade away our authentic freedom in Christ for mists of deception and man-made controls.

Riding the Restoration Horse into the Ground

The belief that God is restoring his church to spiritual wholeness and truth has been persistent in American church history. Among conservative religionists, almost every new direction and misdirection has played with the image in some measure. New movements have consistently ascribed the highest seat in God's great recovery plan to themselves: the Mormon Church, Seventh Day Adventists, the Watchtower Society, the original Pentecostal movement, the New Order of the Latter Rain, the Restoration of David's Tabernacle and, as of late, the New Apostolic Reformation. The paradigm is relentlessly picked up and carried down the line. One must wonder if God will ever wrestle his church from Constantine's hand.

The restoration horse has been ridden to death. The entire idea of a great structural restoration of the church gets overplayed and loses all proportion. Every major campsite along the old Pentecostal trail had at one time crowned itself the defining and final manifestation of the Church of Jesus Christ on earth. But they were always outdone by upstart groups who, leapfrogging over them, snatched the crown and ordained themselves God's most favored ones. Each thought it was to be the ultimate elite company of end-time Spirit-filled overcomers. This aspiration (unholy ambition, I would say) is forever churning the waters in the Pentecostal-Charismatic world.

The restoration motif never wears out because it so beautifully fits the designs and interests of any errant group. It instantly bestows historical significance upon their cause and sets a worldwide mandate before their eyes. Adherents immediately see themselves as the truest followers of God. They are the faithful and favored remnant he has gathered together, powerfully anointed by his Holy Spirit for these last days. They are God's elite corps.

Any novice should be forgiven for being enticed, but those exposed to decades of this story line should have gotten past it years ago. One should consider just how short the shelf life has been for similar claimants. Numerous groups have prophesied great places for themselves in history before their histories even began. Their claims to specific roles in God's great end-time plan for the planet have either faded from the radar or been pushed to the margins with the simple passage of time. Only history itself can make a verdict on what has been restorative and reforming to the Church of Jesus Christ. The proverbial wisdom of 1 Kings 20:11 is timeless: "One who puts on his armor should not boast like one who takes it off." We should not boast of our great contributions and victories until we have truly attained them.

Closing Points to Ponder

Pervasive at ground level in Pentecostal-Charismatic domains is the assumption that God will never use someone in powerful ways if his life and beliefs are not in good order. However, if believers were party to private conversations of their pastors and leaders they would discover how much perplexity and grief is expressed precisely because this does occur. Errant Christians will preach the gospel and people will come to Christ, even when the discipleship that follows is predatory and destructive. Many are amazed at how slowly God seems to deal with certain situations, how long it takes before decisive closure comes. God does not automatically withdraw his power, his presence, and manifestations when error abounds. His goodness and love toward his people of all stripes, and his long-suffering, are enduring.

We can easily mistake God's blessing on our lives and the functioning of his gifts in our ministries for an automatic and personal confirmation that he is pleased with us and his personal favor is resting upon us. But we can misread the screen and so can other people. God's blessing upon our lives does not accurately meter just how pleased he is with us. A gifting from God is not a blanket approval or a spiritual credential for us to wave. It is his enablement on our lives to do some enduring work for the Kingdom of

God. It does not guarantee we are flying on course, are sound in our beliefs, or operating with "clean" hands in our gifts. Observers can make wrong assumptions when they look at us, sometimes to their own detriment. Such blessings are signs that God is *good* to us but they are not proofs that he is altogether pleased with us.

The now-classic *Peter Principle*, where one moves up a ladder of successes until he bottoms out in his own incompetence— neither advancing nor going back—has parallels in our world too. Personality cults are prevalent and trust is deep. One's gifts and callings can lead them, often unfortunately, into other things. The mystic healer and worker of miracles can presume to be a great teacher. The popular teacher without administrative gifts may aspire to pastor a large church. And the competent pastor may reach for the holy grail of apostleship. This can be disastrous when trusting believers follow them into deception or a brick wall.

Unlike their evangelical and mainline counterparts, Pentecostal-Charismatics are much less exposed to good expository preaching and teaching. The best message, for many, is always the most inspirational one. Theme preaching is prevalent, with the listener emerging with memorable impressions of what the pastor said, but not the same clarity on what the cited Bible passages themselves were teaching. Too many read their Bibles superficially yet fully immerse themselves in particular streams of Charismatic literature. This is a lamentable reversal of good counsel to read the Bible intensely and thoroughly, so one can immediately discern departures from the main flow and proportion of Scripture.

Error is never just a flat issue of doctrinal deviation. It is at a deeper and personal level a deviation in our thinking about God and a distortion in our views of ourselves and other people. Error is devious business precisely because it departs from the spirit and content of the Scriptures while purporting to bring them to light. It force-fits the exegesis to get there and introduces its own version of special revelation to jump over the bumps in biblical interpretation.

But the real evil lurks in recasting the package as God's message for the times, pressing everyone into a corner and forcing them to make a decision of ultimate proportions: to remain faithful to God and embrace the fuller "truth," or to reject the message and be shuffled to the margins of God's Kingdom. This clever device is shamelessly perpetuated in the contemporary Pentecostal-Charismatic world.

Chapter Five

Authentic Education or Simple Indoctrination? Whose Thoughts are You Thinking?

Anyone engaged in the pursuit of Christian education should periodically ask themselves a probing question: Am I obtaining sound preparation for my Christian life and ministry, or am I being groomed in a party line and trained for their narrow band of Christian service? Indoctrination hems us in. It is a box that directs the information flow toward specific beliefs and attitudes. Though not immediately apparent, conformity is the primary goal and the education process runs down narrow tracks to get us there. Indoctrination is hard-driving because it seeks full acceptance of its opinions and ideas, and necessarily resorts to drill and repetition to embed its partisan ideas on the mind. This is standard practice in sectarian circles running with a new stream of purported revelation and splinter groups anxiously disassociating themselves from other church groups. It is the predictable methodology of insular Christian worlds in general. The inherent dishonesty lies in the fact that the instructor knows something about both the aims and the process that the student does not.

True education opens itself to critical evaluation and public scrutiny. Its goal is not to convert every mind, nor win every argument, nor track everyone's commitment to the cause. Indoctrination, in contrast, shirks away from scrutiny and leaves little space for independent thinking. The well-known English churchman, John Stott, articulated the distinction:

> Indoctrination is a false education; it is imposing one's mind and one's will on others. True education is stimulation, a catalyst which encourages individuals to make their own responses. (*Understanding the Bible,* 1976)

A real education, I would say, should leave us open to a larger Christian world and make us pliable in our Savior's hands. Indoctrination intentionally limits those horizons and more easily misdirects our loyalties toward human handlers. It invariably diminishes one's life in Christ even as it purports to enlarge it, because along with the biblical and spiritual teachings, it is imposing its own human agenda on the learner. Are we being equipped for the Kingdom or being groomed for the group?

Not the "Hotel California" but Bad Nevertheless

Indoctrination has its own trademarks and can be easily identified. My wife and I, with another couple, once attended a marriage-counselling training seminar at a hotel facility. We were ushered into a meeting room where a good number of couples were already seated and placed on the front line immediately before the presenters. My wife suggested we might sit in a semi-circle so we might see each other but was told the format could not be changed.

The seminar was on full drive from the onset. Session materials were presented at an incredible rate with no interaction, no discussion, and no questions to be asked except on points of clarification. I was finding myself unable to evaluate much of anything before the presentation had moved on to subsequent topics. The information barrage was ceaseless, making it impossible to adequately process. I could not even catch the corner of my wife's eye to see if she too shared my misgivings on several assertions. There was no stopping to collect one's thoughts on any matter and no coming up for air. Every item for the marriage relationship and home life was prescriptive, a rule to be put into practice, and procedures for handling family business were mandated down to the particulars.

A late morning intermission afforded the briefest of interpersonal conversations but I quickly realized the couples in the rows behind us were previously trained counsellors who had been asked to attend these sessions. I sensed some intentional staging had taken place in the seating arrangements and these folk were getting a timely re-immersion into an intensely systematic program. We discovered in the afternoon that the weekly home counselling sessions were to be verbatim presentations of what was drilled into us. The material was to be presented in our homes with no discussion or questions permitted except to clarify points that were presented. No coffee times and no fellowship times were to be provided, and attendees were to be hustled out the door at the close of each session.

These hours became grueling, and by late afternoon my mind was exhausted—but my spirit was churning. We stepped out for a quick meal with our friends where we debriefed and downloaded our concerns. We returned to tell the presenters this was a most pretentious kind of training, nothing more than a canned system of indoctrination and an insult to persons capable of thinking for themselves. And we left.

The excuse that there was so much material and so little time was hollow. This was a systematic program of indoctrination, one that reduced personal Christian counsel to rules that must be followed, and not an authentic education of any kind. The atmosphere was oppressive. Knowing the background of the founders, I suspect they regarded their seminar akin to a "revelation-knowledge," very much God's thing from start to finish, and no one was to tamper with it. Whenever we are convinced everything we have to say is the "truth," the finer points of ethical conduct get glossed over because the end justifies whatever means we use to get there.

Indoctrination and Psychological Conditioning

The foregoing example is particularly crass, but the aggressive mode and rigid structure is not foreign to Pentecostal-Charismatics. Indoctrination is typically undertaken with more subtlety and conducted over a longer period of time. Yet the element of suppressing individual evaluation and inquiry is ever present. On several occasions I have heard leaders instructing congregations not to discuss church matters and concerns with others, but to discuss these issues only with them. This is not without merit but needs to be further defined. This instruction is consistently cast as a protection against malicious gossip and dissension in the body. But it just as easily serves as a gag order preventing members from comparing notes and discussing legitimate issues of concern. Dissension is not the same thing as disagreement. Spiritual unity does not require everybody to always think the leaders' thoughts. D. Johnson and J. VanVonderen speak of "can't talk" relationship systems as a problem in their own right (*The Subtle Power of Spiritual Abuse,* 1991:90). Whenever a spiritually abusive church situation is exposed, a gag-order code of conduct is usually uncovered in the woodwork. It is an essential component in cultivating a climate of control.

Members of the Jim Jones cult were so conditioned not to raise questions about their leaders that even couples were afraid to express misgivings to one another. They suppressed their feelings of distress as the discipline of the children became heavy-handed because nobody else was saying anything, and they no longer trusted their own judgment. People need to be free to think, to speak, and to interact. When we have misgivings, a sense of something wrong, we need to talk to someone else—often someone outside the circle. We do not get our bearings without some external points of reference. When we believe someone else has the spiritual authority to prescribe who we can and cannot speak with, then that alone indicates that somebody has stolen something from us. Insecure, controlling leaders take thousands of Pentecostal-Charismatics half-way to Jonestown with their compelling pitches and indoctrinating methods, and it's usually a minority who suddenly wake up and get themselves out of those situations.

Spiritual Line-Breeding

My uncle raised registered Hereford cattle. He once told me that some breeders get into *line-breeding,* that is, crossing their animals back to near-relatives, and how a few were quite successful at this. The risk, of course, was a genetic throwback, sometimes a dwarf Hereford, which was cute but an obvious discredit to any breeder's reputation. Years later I saw one of these mini-Hereford bulls in a rodeo act, and I have long thought it would make a fitting analogy of spiritual line-breeding, which is too much spiritual DNA from too small a pool. Too much input from too few people in one's spiritual development and discipleship becomes a problem in itself. The limited exposure and tracked thinking are immediately discernable.

Inbred Christian camps work as hard at cultivating loyalty to the group and nurturing elitist attitudes as they do at preparing disciples for faithful service to Christ. "Training" easily becomes preparation to function well within the group, but not necessarily within the larger Christian world. Leadership's watchful care over those in the fold may bring with it a good measure of psychological conditioning. The function and role of leadership is constantly reinforced and paraded, and defining doctrines which distinguish the group are continually projected. Long, sometimes grueling teaching sessions inculcate the faithful in the familiar "truth" essential to maintaining the life of the group and perpetuating the movement.

To deviate from the group and the doctrine is at the least to abandon one's high and lofty calling in God. It is to compromise the very truth of God.

Spiritual line-breeding is deliberate and controlled. Everything comes out of a small, tight circle of influence. More than a few church Bible schools seem prone to this, being founded on some "present truth" with the pastor and a couple associates as core instructors. The gene pool is too limited and too controlled to be considered a bona fide Christian education. Schools that hire too many of their own graduates risk similar consequences. I typically scan the course offerings if I read up on particular Pentecostal-Charismatic schools and colleges. An absence of courses on biblical interpretation, church history, and broad theological understandings, and limited attention to biblical studies, suggests an insufficient interest in laying broad Christian foundations. It indicates too much investment in partisan concerns and little concern with preparing students to evaluate for themselves. How wide is the scope of exposure? A cross-section of reading materials for various courses sometimes tells its own story.

Many schools have a crisp focus on practical ministry, but go lightly, even superficially, on the academic end. I acknowledge the opposite approach begets enormous shortfalls of its own, but I am here pressing the point that the academic component cannot be glossed over and still deliver a solid outcome. I see little enrichment and limited value in knowing no Christian world but our own. A true education should seek to develop lifelong learners who have not only been equipped to read and understand the Bible for themselves, but encouraged and enabled to do much of their own thinking. A great obstacle to Spirit-led living and ministry in the Pentecostal-Charismatic world is the dependent and compliant constituencies who constantly need God's will and God's truth mediated to them through human leaders.

My opinion, given the continual doctrinal undercurrents and confusion brewing beneath the surface, is that ideas of

Pentecostal-Charismatic unity are rather thin and pretentious. We are more sectarian than we imagine ourselves to be. Diverse kingdoms expend incredible effort seeding the minds of their disciples with in-house propaganda and private prejudices against other camps and major Christian denominations. Where is the great effort to establish solid biblical foundations, theological clarity, and clear thinking? Our disciples need these resources if they are to walk through and sort through the confusion and unresolved issues that have long been boiling up. The dilemma with a fortress mentality is that we never know for certain if the wall is there to keep others out—or there to keep us in!

Snaring the Mind with Deductive Logic

Some popular books are aimed broadly to teach and instruct; others are weighted toward inspiration and encouragement. Still others are driven by specific agendas. And some are designed not simply to persuade, but to logically wrestle the reader into a corner. One making a particular case for one stream of the current apostolic restoration caught my attention because of its clever format. This small book was structured like a traditional fish-trap, large in scope, broadly Pentecostal, and inclusive in the opening chapters, but then closing in and logically restricting the reader's wiggle-room. At the end of the book—if they've bought into the logic and biblical interpretations, the authoritative assertions, and the hazy threat of rejecting God's way—they are trapped in a rationally confined space.

The book was designed not merely to shape one's thinking, but to convince them of their need of a personal apostolic covering without which they can neither develop effectively in Christ nor find adequate protection from spiritual powers. In short, one can never fully access the graces and power of God until they link up their personal life with an apostle. By cleverly upgrading the apostolic function to a full intermediary role, the door is opened for the professed apostle to insinuate himself deeply into the believer's personal life. The book employs its own kind of indoctrination strategy. It is crafted to not only track the reader toward an apparently inevitable conclusion, but also to capitalize on some spiritual insecurities. It aims to prepare the reader emotionally and mentally to gladly accept the ring in their nose and "trust"' themselves to an apostle.

Fishing with a "Revelation"

Teaching and learning will ever remain huge components of Christian faith and practice, and indoctrinating methods will never disappear. Within the Pentecostal-Charismatic environment, I am convinced they will never subside because of the pervasive notion of comprehensive revelation-knowledge. This is where a whole package of beliefs is deemed to have been directly sourced from God. Because the whole theology is "truth," there is no place for critical evaluation, only believing and accepting what the Spirit is claimed to be presenting. Proponents feel little obligation to account for their beliefs and assertions. It is for them truth that comes from God, something to be embraced and received, not analyzed. If it is God's business from start to finish, who can dispute it? Who needs to answer for it? And thus, in these camps, indoctrination becomes fully legitimate because it achieves the purposes of God. The abiding myth is that specific church governmental paradigms and particular theological frameworks are divine disclosures and driven by the Spirit of God. This is the big lie to which Charismatic peoples are irresistibly drawn. I see little reflection and few lessons learned—and little hope for Pentecostal-Charismatics on this one.

Final Comments

The more we gravitate toward indoctrination, the more we are diminished and risk a carbon copy education. Indoctrination is teaching for a controlled outcome, and like propaganda in general, seeks to impose its own shape on attitudes and responses. Duplicity is ever-present and there is always something misleading in the process. Indoctrination is not authentic persuasion. Believers nurtured and trained in insular environments who one day realize they have been shorted on a bona fide Christian education—prepared for little more than a future within a narrow elitist group— will be an angry bunch.

This is the acid test: Are you simply being cloned, essentially being taught what to think, or are you at the same time being taught how to process this stuff and encouraged to work it out for yourself? How much guilt and flattery, and social pressure, is coming down the pipes in the learning process? Are you free to disagree on anything more than mere incidentals? Your mind is God's gift to you. Keep your mind open and teachable, but do not let anyone make it a playground for themselves. It is not someone else's personal space—it is yours!

When we have not been out of the circle nor have had significant exposure to those who have, the spiritual air we breathe has always been within a confined space or a defensive huddle. We have learned that only those aligned within the inner network can be true and trusted. We have not learned much.

We make our truest personal choices and deepest commitments in the face of real alternatives to the contrary. Without authentic exposure to a larger Christian world and an assortment of believers and unbelievers who do not think like us, we are not made to think deeply or to wrestle through to our own conclusions. Instead we subscribe—and eat what is put on our plates.

Chapter Six

Thou Shalt Judge Some Things or Wish You Did: Discernment and Disconnects

Diligent believers can be crassly literal with the injunction "Do not judge" (Mathew 7:1), and stretch it to fit all matters pertaining to Christian faith and behavior. Even a dissenting opinion troubles the consciences of some. They endeavor to fulfill Jesus' words by never questioning a claim or a viewpoint, never suspecting someone of contrivance, and never discussing these misgivings with others. Some have been conditioned by their own religious subcultures to run on these tracks. Others have concluded for themselves that taking Jesus seriously simply takes you there. I am certain Jesus is not making such a sweeping statement, that he is directing his words at our edgy remarks about people's motives, our blanket criticism of others, and the condemning spirit with which we speak of them.

I say this because of what immediately follows. Jesus asks why we look at the sawdust speck in our brother's eye and fail to see the plank in our own. It is precisely in our self-righteous scrutiny of someone else that dismissive judgments arise in our hearts and accusations fly off the ends of our tongues. The larger context of the entire New Testament provides an even broader backdrop for putting Jesus' words into perspective. This enables us to see the difference between our judgmental and bitter criticisms of others, and the consistent call of Scripture to make sound judgements. It is for *us* to judge between sound doctrine and bad, between prophetic utterances that are on and those that are off, and to assess our conduct in the light of others, imitating those who walk uprightly and finding some necessary distance from those who do not. Each of these pulls us into the business of making assessments and evaluations, and formulating our own conclusions, which are, if I might mention the word, personal *judgments* on one thing or another.

Discernment

Discernment, in general, is making distinctions, differentiating between the authentic and the counterfeit, the good and the bad, the true and the false. The basic Greek term *krino* means "to judge, to assess," and this root occurs both in "distinguishing (lit. discernings) between spirits" (1 Corinthians 12:10) and "to distinguish good from evil" (Hebrews 5:14). In the first passage, the discernment in view is a *pneumatikon,* a specific manifestation of the Holy Spirit, who—though functioning through human channels—transcends natural human abilities and dispositions. It is a gift of the Spirit that gives an immediate reading of what is driving a person or a situation. The second passage describes a discernment that leans toward the human side of the spectrum, moral and spiritual sensibilities that have been heightened through continual use. Each, in its own way, shapes a judgment because it enables us to make a discriminating call between one thing and another, and provokes a response from us to specific matters, persons, or circumstances.

A "heads-up" from God often comes as a distinct first impression and typically cuts across the grain of anything we might be thinking. I recall receiving an instant insight on one occasion and responding, "No God, these are good people," only to realize soon enough that he knew something I did not. Sometimes discernment brings to us a general caution, at other times an impulse to distance ourselves, at times a specific warning or word of knowledge. I remember one woman considering a particular church because she so enjoyed the worship component yet felt something was wrong, something she could not put her finger on. Still she remained quite intent on returning. She certainly would not have been the first person enticed toward an unhealthy situation by the music and worship. Her failing, I suggest, was her equivocation, her hesitation to act decisively on the discerning signal she had received.

I counsel anyone to embrace an early imprint such as this as a benchmark for future dealings with individuals or church fellowships. It is vital to lock in on those spiritual cues and intuitions, for we may find ourselves facing a barrage of suggestions to the contrary. I have had conversations with believers, some seasoned in ministry, and each of them frustrated because they had received a defining marker and were convinced it was from the Lord—yet in the crunch and amid the distractions of other things had let go of it.

Our sense of smell is analogous to spiritual discernment in general, and the conditioned human dimension in particular. My work has for a long time taken me directly into people's living spaces. Those first few moments always present a sharp olfactory sweep of the premises and things not in view are remarkably clear and nuanced. But that clarity dissipates rapidly as one is acclimatized to that environment. Repetitive experiences and learning to register one's initial takes are invaluable because the real story is sometimes not the one being played out for our eyes and ears. That too is the essence of discernment, making a distinction between what is really going on and what we are being led or leading ourselves to believe.

God faithfully gives us discernment and enough of what we need to know for particular circumstances. We can, however, be casual and reckless in our handling of it, and neither faithful nor competent on our end. We grow in this domain through our immersion into an array of life experiences and some bouncing off the walls. As a young believer, I was hustled by an errant Pentecostal group and remember distinct impressions that something was not right in some of their teachings. But every question I raised was met with pat, convincing interpretations of biblical passages, and I found myself progressively boxed in until I was rationally trapped on all sides. I deduced my inner read was not the voice of God but my own resistance, and I dragged my own unhappy spirit with me into a cultic orb from which I had to be liberated some weeks later.

Previous to this I had sensed a leading toward Bible college but did not see the necessity when the personal presence of God and my church connection seemed sufficient. A quick dip in a Christian cult taught me that God's Spirit is faithful, but I cannot be trusted to get it right every time. He also had no intention of giving me comprehensive one-on-one tutorials. I would always need a broad base of general and biblical knowledge, and diverse inputs from a vast network of mature and informed Christian believers to keep me from losing myself in a hole somewhere and taking someone else with me. And yes, I have been pro-Bible college ever since.

A suspicious disposition is not a gift of discernment or a discerning ability. It is simply a bias, personal and deeply entrenched, that skews our take on everything. Spiritual discernment, despite our common usage, is not inherently negative in tone and content. It also elicits open and positive reactions from us. Our hearts are made immediately responsive to many who are essentially strangers to us. We may intuitively sense a need in someone's life, quite apart from visual cues or conversational hints, but never think of it as spiritual discernment. Further information or a specific word of knowledge may give us clarity to minister, but the initial spiritual impulse that was positive and open-hearted prepped us to step forward and do something.

My initial experiences of being in someone's presence and being suddenly overtaken by emotions of intense dislike for them left me feeling guilty and confused, and scrambling to regain my emotional composure. Similarly, dropping in on services at unfamiliar churches has sometimes surprised me with an irrepressible agitation in my spirit, and the impulse to leave quickly and quietly. Over time I have learned to work with this. Intimately knowing my personal zones, in particular, my own biases and prejudices, my normal criteria for liking and disliking people, and my normal emotional responses to people and situations plays a crucial role. These are my own human filters and radars for processing incoming information, and I know what sets me off. But in my experience, a discerning insight of a revelatory sort, mediated directly from God's Spirit to my spirit, does not register on these radars. And without any analysis or emotional processing, that bit of information can suddenly be present in my conscious mind demanding that I deal with it. Knowing my "normals" (and being honest with them) provides a baseline and some calibration to distinguish when it is mostly God's Spirit and when it is mostly my own.

We learn to give ourselves permission to believe—based on an inner insight before the evidence is apparent—that some persons are not authentic, some are up to no good, and others are packing an unclean spirit or have a dark band running through their souls. Seasoned deceivers become smooth operators, presenting a convincing Christian life and displaying apparent soundness. But we teach ourselves, when God gives us a discerning insight, to hold our ground and not to cave to our own overly-sensitive consciences. Serious error is often *felt* first. Clarity typically comes but we may have to wait for pieces to shuffle into place. And sometimes it is best to wait quietly. Discernment is typically given in capsule insights and the full story emerges later—and sometimes not at all.

Discernment is crucial and we ignore it at our own peril. If God is telling us something is wrong, then something really is wrong despite appearances and a mix of other impressions. But putting it all together is not strictly a spiritual enterprise. Much of it is picked up at ground level with eyes wide open. Be very aware of the "disconnects," for they too afford a read on what is occurring beneath the surface.

Beware of the Disconnects

Disconnects are not quirks and minor oddities. Neither are they simply spiritual immaturities. Disconnects are big holes and discrepancies in people's lives, grave contradictions between the Christian life they are presenting and the one they are living. Typically concealed from view, they cross our paths as "pop-ups."

Jesus told us, "No good tree bears bad fruit, nor does a bad tree bear good fruit. Each tree is recognized by its own fruit" (Luke 6:43-44). We can be fooled by trusting too much too soon, and walking about with our eyes closed. Not everything about piecing a picture together is mystical and intuitive. The basic observation of life gives us glimpses into people's lives, and at times we see disparities of much greater consequence than specks in our brothers' eyes.

Integrity is the baseline of authentic Christian living. The term describes a certain wholeness and completeness in one's person. If someone is integrated he is soundly "fitted together" and his real life is not a trail of loose ends. And the important marker is this: he is not driven to reinvent himself for public consumption. The person we see is essentially the person they are.

Personal gifts and talents are more immediately visible than inner life and character. We all project our strengths in social situations, but caution bells should ring with the relative stranger who oversells himself and aggressively pursues our trust. This suggests an agenda not fully on the table. People can be too helpful, too intimate, and too determined to have a personal relationship with us. They strive too much to impress and to woo us, and to make it happen. Such persons are actively carving out a sphere of influence for themselves, looking for a role in our personal lives or a stepping stone to a role in our fellowship. We read these social disconnects quite apart from knowing the designs beneath them.

This is our early warning system and the stage to break it off. And this is the juncture where timid souls choke because their sensitive consciences will not permit them to be blunt or rude. They are compelled to be nice and seldom do they trust their own judgment. Feeling duty-bound to give everyone the endless benefit of the doubt, they do not hustle out of situations when they should. And this is compounded when the individual before them is bold, confident, and by all appearances has done nothing wrong. Some intrusive situations are best addressed with a final word and a quick exit, for there can never be a socially smooth and comfortable way to close it off.

So beware of the disconnects, the strained socializing behaviors, and mounting discrepancies between what a person is and how they present themselves. These are easily disregarded. The preoccupation with presentation should grab our attention. Without some history together, the truest self, the real person on the inside is not an easy or immediate read. We need time to get to know the person on the inside, just as others require time to know the authentic us.

Clever people exploit the general climate of trust and openness in Christian circles for their own ends. They do much harm when they ingratiate themselves into the personal and corporate lives of a fellowship, or draw away disciples for themselves. We ought to pay attention to significant "disconnects" in people's lives because they frequently belie some secret life or private agenda. And when the gaps become too big to believe what is being played out before our eyes—don't!

Chapter Seven

Sticking with the "Script" of Scripture: Read It the Way It is Written

A neighbor lady, with whom I have one or two conversations a year, walked over to the fence a few years ago and asked me, "How's your honey?" "Doing fine," I answered (assuming she was referring to my wife). "Do you need another one?" she asked. I responded rather slowly and defensively, "No . . . I already have one." We looked at each other strangely. Just as she asked, "Do you know what I am talking about?" I suddenly remembered she had given me a small pail of Alberta honey the previous year. Much to my relief, I realized she was simply asking if I wanted another one. She had a specific frame of reference in mind when she struck up the conversation—but I did not. The cues and the clues in her words did not register, and I had moved rapidly to my own assumptions about what she meant. For a few moments I was lost. I had no context at all to interpret what she was saying. I was, for an eternity of mere seconds, blindly sifting through her words and trying to connect the dots, but without a context for what she was saying, the meaning was beyond me.

Without Context We Don't Get the Message

Context is the environment in which events occur (historical-cultural context), and it is the setting in which words are spoken or written (literary context). If there is one guideline for reading and understanding the Bible that is indispensable, it is this one. Almost all skewed interpretation begins with a disregard for the immediate context.

Those adept at reading the context in a conversational discourse and newspaper stories, and following a debate on CNN, often exempt themselves when it comes to reading their Bibles. They would never think of taking phrasing and terminology from one part of a magazine article and jamming it up against a paragraph in a different article simply because it contains two identical words. Nor would they leapfrog from one sentence on one page to another sentence on a different page. So why do sensible and capable persons quickly abandon the familiar conventions of language and communication, and attention to context, when they read the Scriptures?

They do it simply because, whether they have thought about it or not, they bring an entirely different set of assumptions to the Bible. They do not stop to reflect that God guided ordinary human agents to use their everyday man-made languages to disclose himself and his salvation. The Father sent Jesus not just to die and rise again, but to be a tangible and visible close-up of what he is like—"God with a face," someone has said. God made himself available to us in ways we humans normally receive information and understand things in our world. He drew close to us to reveal himself in understandable language, not conceal himself behind riddles and cryptic messages, as some seem determined to prove. Indeed, the very idea of "God's Word" sets many off on a personal quest for anything *except* what is printed on the page in front of them.

Dealing Ourselves a Hand of Cards

Common practice is readers hopscotching around from one verse to another on the assumption that each passage is its own little thought capsule. And many Bible verses do have a crisp and understandable message in a small and convenient package. Still, just about all of them are found in the Bible with verses leading up to them and verses following. Even they are pieces of a broader picture, one chunk in the natural flow and development of a line of thought. What leads into a passage and what follows casts a light on what is being said. Taken together with the other verses in the "surround" they give us the larger view and the main message.

Older Bibles for sure printed individual verses as if each were its own little paragraph, and this obscured connections between verses to some degree. Someone suggested the first step to interpretation is to disregard modern chapter and verse divisions. Everything from verse numbers to punctuation and word spacing are editorial helps added for clarity, ease of reading, and conformity with the language of translation. They are not there in the early Biblical manuscripts. Modern translations, with their paragraphing aids, do much to get us reading and thinking about Scripture in larger frames of reference.

Going Quasi-Occultic

The full-flip from the natural sense and meaning of language (the "literal" sense normally, but not always) to an intensely mystical interpretation is a different game altogether. Context means nothing here, and the meaning of particular verses and phrases has nothing to do with the quest this reader is on. Here, any purpose of the Scriptures lies far beyond the seemingly ordinary language in which it is written. What they are looking for is not even *in* the Bible. They are fishing for something from the spiritual realms to be channelled to them *through* the Bible. Most look for personalized messages and directives from God, and the Bible becomes at most a medium for them. The written Word of God is conceived as spiritual jello facilitating communications from the invisible heavenly realms.

Formulating Spiritual Allegories

"Spiritualizing," while not as extreme as the foregoing, has only a minor interest in the literal meaning of Bible passages. Here too the reader is looking for "truth" or "spiritual knowledge" to be disclosed to them by some other venue than the plain meaning of words and sentences. The real meat of the Word, for them, is in its purported spiritual meaning, the allegorical interpretation that unveils the *hidden* truth beyond the natural meaning. The obvious difficulty is that there is no controlling process that comes with it, no manual with a place to begin or a place to stop. Forsaking the natural sense of language in Bible study for spiritualizing modes of interpretation invariably results in someone reading novel theological views back into the Bible. The million dollar question, of course, revolves around who gets to be that special someone. The teaching authority in the Roman Church has long endorsed certain spiritual and allegorical interpretations of Scripture beyond the literal, and many contemporary Pentecostal-Charismatic circles have borrowed their spiritualizing "exegesis" directly from the earlier Latter Rain movement.

But spiritualized interpretations can never be objectively evaluated nor validated. They are simply carried by a claim to apostolic spiritual authority of some sort, and can never be confirmed by anyone else—only believed or not believed, accepted or rejected. On this wavelength, interpretation and meaning become arbitrary because they do not come from the words and sentences from the Bible. They do not even come *from* the Bible. They come from the official interpreter for the group, be it the apostolic authority vested in the Roman Church or the diversity of apostolic authorities in the Charismatic churches.

Spiritualized "Eisegesis"—Going Whithersoever the Pilot Taketh Thee

The phrase has common usage but the idea of a "spiritualizing exegesis" is an oxymoron, a contradiction in itself, because "exegesis" means to draw something *out,* whereas spiritualizing is always us putting our own thoughts *into* the Scripture. Spiritualizing is more accurately "eisegesis," reading something into the text. Years ago, in a magazine article, a spokesman for the Restoration of David's Tabernacle movement set forth his fundamental principle for interpreting Scripture. He cited a passage where the apostle Paul describes how our natural bodies will be transformed into glorified spiritual bodies at the resurrection: "Howbeit that was not first which is spiritual but that which is natural; and afterward that which is spiritual" (1 Corinthians 15:46, KJV). This for him contained the key: first the natural, then the spiritual. This was his general guiding rule for proper biblical interpretation. The true understanding of Scripture, he said, is cradled in God using natural things to teach us about invisible, eternal realities. And therefore everything written in the Old Testament is essential for understanding the New.

The point about the Old Testament is overplayed, but not without merit. Numerous parallels between the natural experiences of Old Testament believers and the spiritual journeys of New Testament saints are readily observed. In retrospect, we discern many allusions and foreshadows of New Covenant realities in the Jewish Scriptures.

However, the author of this article was reaching for something far beyond these. He was defending an all-encompassing rationale for trumping literal biblical interpretation with his spiritualizing interpretation—and deriving his theology from that. And he was forcing it from a Bible passage and context that says nothing about interpreting Scripture. Among earlier proponents of the New Order of the Latter Rain and the later Restoration of David's Tabernacle, the spiritualizing of Old Testament narratives and religious culture is intensive and detailed. The process far exceeds the widely accepted typology and foreshadowing in Scripture. Much of the old Pentecostal preaching was given to typological and spiritualized interpretation, but the largest element was Christ-centered. Even the old preacher who thought he saw a shadow of Jesus in the tent pegs of the tabernacle was not doing much harm to Jesus. If one was stuck with a particular set of eyeglasses for reading the Bible, the I-see-Jesus ones would probably be the safest and soundest ones to have.

But "spiritual interpretation" in the contemporary Pentecostal-Charismatic world is not primarily focused on Christ at all—the spotlight is consistently on the special people of God, as it was in earlier Latter Rain theology. The group, the faithful remnant, is always the specific object of their own theology. Allegorical feeders converge in a grand picture of themselves front and center in God's final plans for this world, over against the backdrop of unbelieving multitudes who have rejected their message. They are the defining people of God in these last days, the *true* church within the church and the specific fulfillment of the prophesied "Restoration of David's Tabernacle." Spiritualized interpretation in the Pentecostal-Charismatic sphere is consistently a double-edged sword, redefining who is among the faithful and who is not. It fabricates biblical grounds to exalt and imagine great things about the "group," and it finds warrant to regard Christian brothers and sisters who have not bought into the teaching as spiritually substandard. Any inquirer should consider where these particular skews are taking them before they board these trains. Once the final destination for the ride comes into full view, Charismatics in general may realize they want nothing to do with these self-serving, *crème de la crème* "theologies."'

The shortfall in spiritualizing is only the inner circle uncritically buys into it. When pressed to account for their views on specific passages to a larger Christian world, the interpreter has little to appeal to as biblical evidence. He is compelled to appeal to a dubious and unconvincing "revelation" of the Spirit. There is no reasonable discussion that could take place. *Context* is nothing to the spiritual allegorist because he is pressing his own message on the text.

The Final Pitch for "Context"

Analyzing thought is different than analyzing chemical compositions or mathematical formulations. Thought is more fluid and word meanings are not rigidly fixed like numerical values. There are no precise formulas, but there are certainly guiding principles, and as already suggested, the most fundamental yet oft-neglected benchmark is that a sentence or a verse needs to be understood in its context.

Many readers are very literal in their approach to the Bible but treat the whole of Scripture as though it were one large and level landscape. Thus they move from the Old Testament to the New, and from one book of the Bible to another, without even shifting a gear. Context is neglected and easily dismissed because they see God alone as the author of it all, having essentially "dictated" what was written. The human side of the equation, in many minds, is of little consequence because the writers are viewed as passive instruments in the hand of God. These assumptions make it easy to deductively stitch together passages from different places, whether they have an apparent connection or not.

Word studies can get wooden and superficial when we presume a word used to mean one thing in one passage means the same thing when used elsewhere. Leaping through the Bible after a theme, when it becomes our general approach, leaves us impoverished because we never stop to tap into the Bible's own flow of thought and follow it through. We are continually running off on our own trails. Most books of the Bible were written one sentence after another, and to know what the Bible is saying, we must read it one sentence after another. It has been said that the meaning and message of Scripture is found mostly in its phrases, sentences, and paragraphs—and not so much in individual words. The more context we have, the more clarity we have, because the surroundings shape and shade the meanings of key words.

The mystic interpreter is enticed by the aura of a mysterious deeper meaning beyond the text, and spiritual allegorists consistently transpose their own beliefs into the Scriptures. In abandoning the natural sense of language in Bible study, they are forsaking the only platform where the Bible has a consistent message for all people everywhere. The meaning of Scripture *now* has to be what it was when it was first written down. This is the only universal baseline for understanding Scripture itself, and then we must make *our* applications from there. Aim for the natural sense of Scripture, which is to say, words and phrases mean what they usually meant in that time and culture. Contexts (historical, cultural, literary) are not magic bullets for interpretation, but they keep tracking us in the right direction, moving us deeper into the Bible text itself. Context is fundamental because it makes us look at an entire line of thought. This is "knowing" the Bible.

Read the Scriptures and keep reading them like they are written—and think contextually! That is where most of the cues to meaning are. The biggest step we can make to clean up our handling of Scripture is to home in on the "surrounds," the immediate and overall contexts in which Bible passages occur. Then we can begin to see the true colors and taste the full, natural flavors—instead of smothering them with *our* favorite assortment of spices.

Chapter Eight

The Obsession with Submission and Authority: Disproportion, Grand Distortion, or Spiritual Bullying?

The Pentecostal-Charismatic movement has for decades been consumed with the question of church governance and the theme of "Submission and Authority." There is an historical context for that. But without knowing something of how theology is handled and how it gets boosted in this culture, one might never understand how something like "submission and authority" could become such a fundamental tenet in Charismatic belief and practice.

Here in a Pentecostalized Charismatic world, theological thinking is rarely kept at the level of a better way, or simply a more biblically informed way of doing something. New items are heated up in layers of spiritual spin and scaled up to God's way of doing it. Theological issues become spiritually supercharged and falsely transposed into issues of faith and obedience, and individuals are confronted with the decision to accept or reject the new message God is giving. An incredible burden is foisted on sincere, ordinary believers, now that God's pleasure or displeasure hovers over what they do with the new theological paradigm. Quite apart from the content, this methodology is devilish business and spiritual bullying.

New theologies, overarching in their assertions and infused with divine authority, are powerful religious forces. They lay their claim on everyone because it is now God's program. It is "present truth." Various takes on submission and authority are classic examples of this game, and to this day keep the issue hot on the burner. Theological agendas, because of the spin, are the dominating drivers in these domains.

An Historical Capsule on Submission and Authority

In the formative years, denominationally-detached components of the Charismatic movement lacked solid leadership, church experience, and biblical teaching. Confusion abounded and groups could unravel as quickly as they had formed. Without strong leadership to collect, disciple, and channel the results of the renewal, the movement had real prospects of derailing itself. And anything less than strong, disciplined leadership would have been bowled over in the tide.

Specific historical forces were already converging toward top-down governmental models from several directions. Pastors and mature believers with mainline Pentecostal backgrounds often held a shared aversion to the governmental structures of their former churches. Those wounded and frustrated by district superintendents and congregationally elected boards resolved never to be subject to those systems again. Many congregations did not have a competent pool of elders to choose from in any case, and pastors typically had to disciple and train leaders for roles in their churches. And a generation of converts from a hippie world and generally rebellious youth culture also sent those ministries scrambling to establish principles of order, discipline, and submission to spiritual authorities.

Submission and authority models in the larger Charismatic world were still experimental into the '70s. Watchman Nee books were popular and some themes from the earlier Latter Rain movement, particularly the "fivefold ministry" banner, were being carried forward also. Pentecostal-Charismatics of all stripes adopted that phrasing to distinguish ministry callings (apostles, prophets, evangelists, pastors, and teachers). But not all understood the spiritual authority structure, the church governance, and ideas about appropriate submission that the Latter Rain had invested in their fivefold ministry paradigm. The Restoration of David's Tabernacle and certain other circles did. Most Pentecostals and Charismatics put the emphasis on "ministry functions," but the originators spoke of "ministry offices," and they meant business. For them the five offices were God's precise *method* for bringing Christians to their maturity in Christ. Embossed on a crest in one church's foyer, I saw their model of authority on bold display, in descending order: God the Father, Jesus the Son, the Holy Spirit, Apostles, Prophets, Evangelists, Pastors, and Teachers.

By the early '80s, the well-known "Shepherding" movement was receiving much attention. This rested on very direct influences from the "Fort Lauderdale Five": Derek Prince, Bob Mumford, Charles Simpson, Don Basham, and Ern Baxter, who in the aftermath of someone's moral failing, covenanted to be personally accountable to each other. Their paradigm and practice incorporated two key principles: subjecting one's private life to penetrating scrutiny by his peers and consulting with them on major life decisions. Their teachings and pyramid networking were popular and influential in shaping discipleship-leadership models in many churches, but submission was pushed in many sectors to the point of imposition.

Limits of spiritual authority were consistently ill-defined and open-ended. Church adherents were personally accountable to leadership, but leadership at the highest levels were not accountable to their congregations, only to their own circle of "office-holding" co-equals. Wives uncomfortable with their husband's expectations no longer felt free to object, and employees were boxed in by New Testament injunctions to slaves. Together with authoritative intrusions by pastors in life directions, career choices, marriage matters, and family business, these culminated in widespread reaction to what detractors now tagged "Heavy Shepherding." Much personal tragedy ensued in so short a time. Many of these leaders never took stock but others did. The original "Five" parted company in the mid-eighties following the backlash and a deadlock on a major personal decision. I attended a conference where one was the keynote speaker. When asked about his current stance on submission and accountability, he simply said, "Live with your theology long enough and you will change it." This person publicly repented of his involvement with the shepherding philosophy. The unfortunate reality is that thousands never knew they had the option to see it simply as a "theology," a man-made frame with Bible verses and human logic hung on the hooks. It had been presented to them as God's specific will for them—complete with the personal intrusion and the heavy hand.

The "Error" Issue in Submission and Authority

Error is rarely a bald lie. It is more likely a mix of biblical truths and not-so-blatant departures, creeping along by degrees. The predictable pattern is a chain of subtle distortions that keep collecting, and only late in the day does a deviation from the general picture in Scripture clearly stand out. I once heard an older preacher making the point that "truth" is never just a matter of having the facts, but having them in the right proportions too. He used the illustration of our own faces which not only have numerous components but also have them in proportionate relationship to each other. If our lips kept growing throughout our entire lives, our faces would become gruesomely distorted and a healthy functioning life would become impossible. Biblical proportion is crucial to sound interpretation. Scriptural injunctions are easily isolated from their immediate contexts and relationships to other truths. They can be inflated beyond proportion and recast in an array of applications that were never in the original field of view. The bottom line is this: How biblical is something that ends up miles down the road from the original frames of reference in which the Bible has spoken of it?

The perpetuation of familiar submission and authority paradigms within the Charismatic movement is a classic illustration of error by disproportion. A full-fledged doctrine of submission and a prescriptive hierarchical authority has been artificially grown without a lot of solid New Testament evidence. That big picture is not the general picture in the New Testament churches. How do a few exhortations directed specifically to believers end up making personal "submission" the buzzword and banner slogan to live by in so many churches? The short answer is this: It is not the Scriptures themselves; it is the human drivers behind the doctrines.

As a case study for New Testament interpretation, the submission-authority issue draws attention to several interpretative flaws. One, already alluded to, is adding one seemingly reasonable conclusion to another until we have walked out on a long plank, far from the biblical support with which we started. Our Scriptural case becomes too diluted to carry itself. Another shortfall is the skewed interpretation of biblical imperatives to give them a more authoritarian tone and texture than they really have. Third is the perception of the Bible in its entirety as one large, flat pancake which can be sliced up into pieces and simply reassembled into theologically convenient arrangements as we choose. This handling of Scripture has no practical sense of the progressive nature of biblical revelation and no up-shifting when passing from the Old Testament into the New. Elements from Old Covenant authority models are imported rather loosely and applied without due discrimination to believers under a new covenant. The final recourse for Pentecostal-Charismatics, of course, when the Bible does not hand us what we are looking for, is to dodge careful biblical interpretation altogether and simply declare our beliefs to be a timely revelation from God.

Going Over the Edge on Our Doctrinal Scaffolds

Berkeley Mickelsen, in his classic text on reading and understanding the Bible, describes clearly and simply how the subtle power of extension creeps in and leads us astray. The Scriptures might present a particular statement, and it seems logical and natural to us that this statement coupled with others logically leads us to a further conclusion. This further conclusion leads to still another, and soon we are far removed from that first clear biblical statement (*Interpreting the Bible,* 1963*)*. This may be an old book, but the author's observation is not stale-dated. I have seen this played out many times and have done it myself. "We must not use rationally invented links to give us artificial wholeness" (Mickelsen, p. 348).

This is how we walk out on a plank and lose continuity with the Bible. Blinded by the apparent strength of our own argument, which seems flawless to us, we rarely get back to the solid Scriptural platform from which we started. We rely on "hard" rationalizing to carry us through, when what we really need is "hard" evidence.

The biblical themes of submission, authority, and discipleship have been subjected to precisely this kind of interpretative juggling. Human relationships of every kind require practical submission and structure. We are dysfunctional without them. How much more the Church of Christ? Every believer is enjoined to submit themselves to those who are over them in the Lord because this is foundational to our corporate spiritual life. But in the Charismatic context, *submission* and *authority* are packed full of very precise content and become trigger words which provoke specific responses. This indicates something has been set in place that far exceeds the inferences in the New Testament and its overall depiction of how churches operated in that world.

We go too far out and make assumptions that are not on the biblical horizon. Yet there we stay, adamant that the whole package is Scriptural and therefore a clear expression of God's will, and something to project onto God's people. The Bible never envisions frontline church dogma and strict codes of Christian conduct being raised up around this theme, but Charismatic popularizers and church leaders have made it just that.

Barking with the Imperative Mood

Even competent Greek scholars have sometimes stated that the imperative mood in the language signals a command, and essentially left it at that. I once heard the well-known Pentecostal scholar, Gordon Fee, raise a question about how we use biblical imperatives, making the point they are many times in the New Testament given in a spirit of counsel and encouragement, and not framed as new laws from God. Given my own Pentecostal roots this resonated with me. Grammatical imperatives are often not commands at all. Imperative sentences are repeatedly used in normal language to give an exhortation, give permission, or express a wish. When I say to my wife, "Kiss me, Babe," my words are grammatically constructed as an imperative, but what I am saying is not a command or expectation. It is an overture, essentially a request or invitation. Similarly, "Excuse me" is in fact an apology and "Don't cry" is a consolation.

When Paul in his letters says, "Live in peace with each other" or "Be filled with the Spirit," is he dictating divine orders, or is he giving positive encouragement and godly exhortation to put these things into practice? The grammatical construction itself does not carry the day, but the immediate context infers a particular tone and intention, one that is obviously pastoral and encouraging. This disposition is also present in the classic submission passages: "Respect those who work hard among you, who are over you in the Lord and who admonish you" (I Thessalonians 5:12) and "Obey your leaders and submit to their authority. They keep watch over you as men who must give an account. Obey them so that their work will be a joy, not a burden . . ." (Hebrews 13:17). This instructive counsel was directed to specific parties. It was never intended to give leaders a mandate to induce compliance and personal submission to themselves.

Heavy Shepherding established itself through Pharisaical imposition, and Charismatic believers in their charge were beaten down with biblical imperatives. Discipleship models have adapted over time, but wherever submission and authority are dominant motifs, Scriptural disproportion is locked in. And biblical imperatives will always be systematically applied to squeeze believers into their respective places, even when the process is advanced with gentler tones and a softer voice.

Very few New Testament passages are the hammer of God into which some preachers have transformed them. Even though there is real expectation of following through, the heaviness or lightness of the hand is easily discerned in the context of what is being said. Biblical imperatives make an appeal to move and motivate the human spirit—not to crush it, merely conform it or guilt it into compliance. The same cannot be said of those who have used it to establish dominance and control. The injunction to submit ourselves to those who are over us in the Lord is both personal and functional, but it is not a call to give our unqualified personal allegiance to anyone or surrender our very souls to their personal jurisdictions.

Waving the "Touch Not God's Anointed" Banner

It is not surprising that the model and disposition of Old Testament leadership holds some appeal to Pentecostal-Charismatic leadership. Unlike their counterparts in the early Pentecostal movement, Pentecostal-Charismatics in the late 1900s never fused into just a few major denominations. To this day, an array of smaller fiefdoms, larger kingdoms, networks and alliances, and some denominations are scattered across the landscape. Many resemble insular city-states, each with their own rulers.

But using Old Testament themes to shore up New Testament leadership quickly goes soft at the bottom. Kingship in Israel affords a brilliant cluster of Messianic images and prophecies of the great King and branch of David reigning in justice and righteousness. But it does not advance a leadership paradigm for anyone except Jesus. The historical context from which kingship arose confirms it was a worldly model of power, one that captured the hearts and imagination of the Israelites, and one to which God reluctantly conceded.

Under the system of the "Judges" the individual was never fully autonomous, but they had a large measure of personal freedom. God's concern with kingship was expressed in terms of that loss of freedom and the hardship it would bring to his people. His reluctance was focused on the abusive and exploitive hand that commonly attends such absolute power: heavy taxation, conscription for royal service, and seizures of lands for the king's use. Despite its vulnerabilities, the former system represented some things that were both valued by God and threatened by the introduction of kingship.

Nevertheless, when kingship was established, God honored the program and the king was indeed *God's anointed.* Together with a small circle of other anointed ones, namely priests and prophets who heard from God and to whom divine direction was given, the king ruled the country and divine directives were passed down to administrators and to the people at large.

But hauling components of this wagon indiscriminately across the New Testament border makes faulty assumptions about New Testament leadership and faulty assumptions about the spiritual transition into New Testament reality. The New Covenant is a game changer precisely because it introduces two bold and transforming dimensions. Firstly, every believer has the Holy Spirit in them, and although they may be neither called nor gifted for leadership, they have been given real capacities to know and evaluate spiritual things. The Holy Spirit bears witness to their spirits too, whether something is from God or not, even when it comes from a purported prophet or apostle. Every believer in Christ can come boldly and confidently into the presence of God and there are no human intermediaries that can disrupt that—unless he is led to believe they can. Leaders are in some sense "God's anointed," but not in the absolute sense of an Israelite king, because today every believer also has God's anointing and his living presence in their lives. And God himself exercises his own direct governance of their personal lives through his Holy Spirit without consulting their spiritual overseers. God speaks to them and he gives them direction, and they know him intimately and personally. They have been given much spiritual autonomy, and this is why they have real freedom in Christ. God is personally with them, and they are not at all caught in the same relationship of spiritual dependency that enveloped the Old Testament believer.

Secondly, the average believer today not only has the Scriptures in his hands, but has the ability to understand their import as well. Yes, he needs pastors and teachers too, but not because their gifts are always spiritually enlightening. Sometimes they simply know more about the Bible, more about Christian life and ministry, and have more spiritual experience than they do. The New Testament writings are consistently directed to believers in general, not just their leaders, as those who are fully capable of making spiritual assessments and making their own spiritual judgments on matters that affect them.

These two features—the personal presence of the Living God in every believer and the understandable, written Word of God in their hands—must be given their due. Taken together with explicit biblical statements about our equality in Christ, these two New Covenant features should temper and offset the unbridled assent of leadership in the Pentecostal-Charismatic movement. These distinctive New Testament realities should "democratize" our attitudes and beliefs about ourselves and other believers, and they should produce radical adjustments in our behaviors and relationships. Our church governance models should be *serving* the interests of

New Testament spiritual realities—instead of *imposing* their own little spiritual realties on those in their care.

But too many myths about spiritual leadership have been perpetuated throughout the Pentecostal-Charismatic world, and the over-and-under mentality has been grossly exaggerated. Being "equals" in Christ is meant to have real implications at ground level too. We all should have some real accountability to each other. Yes, the contemptuous upstart who conspires against spiritual leadership is touching "God's anointed," but the spiritual leader who manipulates and insinuates his personal authority into the believer's personal space is also inappropriately touching "God's anointed."

Incredible disparity between laity and leadership was an inevitable given in the formative years of the Charismatic movement. However, many decades later, wherever this is brazenly apparent, it suggests perpetual immaturity and lifelong dependency. It also implies a leadership determined to rule over the Church of Christ like the kings of the Gentiles rule over their kingdoms and lord it over their subjects (Luke 22:25).

Chapter Nine

Tip-Offs on Cults and Cultic Charismatic Churches: If It Looks Like a Duck . . .

We may think people get entangled in cults simply because they are not as smart as the average bear, but it has been repeatedly demonstrated that the typical cult convert is quite intelligent. But they tend to be spiritually aspiring and emotionally needy as well, and it is the combination that makes them vulnerable. What is a "cult?" That depends on what definition we are using. In the broadest sense, any religious system is a "cult" or a "cultus." Nevertheless, in popular usage, a cult was for a long time distinguished simply on the basis of its doctrinal beliefs and departures from orthodox Christian theology. In recent decades, however, attention and popular usage of the word "cult" has shifted to sociological models which focus attention on the human relational dynamics and the measure of control exerted over adherents.

When former Scientology and Children of God adherents are interviewed in television documentaries, the heart of the conversation always moves to the discussion about control—control of information and exposure to ideas, control of the social context, and control of the emotional climate. This paradigm shift is profoundly significant because it targets the crux of the issue, the underlying experience of spiritual abuse and manipulation. It makes us realize that a Christian Church which presents itself as orthodox in its fundamental beliefs many also be cultic in its functional corporate life. Cults are not necessarily "out there" somewhere. A religious organization given to extreme beliefs and practices is readily tagged as a cult, but something closer to generic Pentecostal-Charismatic faith easily slips beneath the radar. Yet adherents in both may share a near-identical experience of manipulative mental and social control.

I have had many conversations with someone who for many years was deeply involved in a Jesus People church which had a strong shepherding-discipleship philosophy. Deeply impressed by popular teachings on submission and authority, he landed on their doorstep when he was sixteen, asking who he should submit to—and he left seventeen years later. I knew something of this church and their reputation for street witnessing and fruitful evangelism. But when I attended a service on one occasion, I sensed there was beneath the exuberant praise and intense energy something seriously askew. I was spiritually agitated, and although at the time I could not precisely identify what it was, I resolved not to return. I had been scalded once before for suppressing my spiritual misgivings.

Many of those gaps were filled in over subsequent years. In several conversations with members of this church, I noted they consistently postured themselves above me and kept detached. I also learned something of the expectations and rules that governed the ship. Single people were expected to reside in their group homes and be discipled under house leaders. Pastoral endorsements were needed for dating and marriage, and every aspect of life was framed by the principle of submission. Ironically, the church still kept a token affiliation with the main Pentecostal fellowship I was with, but they did not mix with other local churches. They were their own world, and the calendar of events and weekly activities kept them constantly circling around themselves.

My friend undoubtedly observed over the years the exodus of many who had rejected the yoke of authority. But his turning point came as he was preparing himself to specifically witness to Jehovah's Witnesses, researching the Watchtower Society, studying their literature and associating with an ex-Witnesses support group. He began to see correspondences between the Watchtower organization and the church to which he and his wife had long been committed. He realized that his own church was just as controlling, just as cultic, and just as insistent on personal submission to its scale of leadership as the Watchtower Society. This realization was his eureka moment, and seeing a fellow adherent thrown out the front door and down the steps for not submitting clinched his decision. Shortly thereafter, he and his wife, of their own volition, went out the door too.

What follows are compact summaries of prevalent cultic trademarks, and these are surprisingly universal. My categories are substantially the same as those one would find in any general introduction to the world of cults.

Cultic Groups have Undisclosed Agendas

There is much masking and misrepresentation in their initial encounters. Impressions are sown which do not accurately or fully disclose their beliefs and functional spiritual life. People are drawn into their world one step at a time, and recruitment strategies are remarkably similar and well-honed. There is first the coming alongside to befriend, then the subtle undermining and discrediting of one's present spiritual loyalties and the process of socially alienating the subject from their normal relationships. A cloud of emotional unsettledness and confusion is created, and against this misty backdrop, new beliefs are planted and nurtured. New clarity has been introduced and the anxiety levels out. Cults crawl into people's lives by instalments and the big picture, the inner reality, is only unfolded as one moves deeper into the system.

Cultic Groups have Authoritarian Leadership Structures

The strong central authority is always on parade and their purported divine appointment is constantly reinforced in the eyes of the people. Almost invariably, this model is the classic hierarchical pyramid, extremely well-defined and boldly set forth. Systematic indoctrination cleverly and subtly displaces personal evaluation and thinking for oneself. Beliefs, behaviors, lifestyles, and relationships are prescribed in detail, and the highly regulated inner religious culture is one that perpetuates dependency and conformity, not personal freedom and individual competency.

Cultic Groups Rely on Non-Biblical Sources of Authority

The real touchstone is always a claim to a new revelation, a pathway to deeper spirituality, or a recovery of the real truth of Scripture. In actual practice, writings and pronouncements of their spiritual authorities become the final word, while plain statements of the Bible are muted or reinterpreted in a specific mold to support the agenda. Personal direct access to God is systematically blunted by either clouding the Bible's ability to speak for itself or convincing adherents they really are unable to correctly interpret the Bible for themselves. In either case, the intervention of leadership severs one's direct access to the Scriptures for themselves, limits their independent access to God, and curbs their ability to think their own thoughts.

Cultic Groups Maintain a Tightly-Closed Belief System

Cultic groups are not particularly concerned with a careful evaluation of evidence because it is already settled that their beliefs are the "truth." Psychological conditioning is systematic and affords the cult increasing control over the minds and lives of its followers. External points of reference are progressively cut off and individuals, deprived of feedback from the outside and friends on the outside, become conditioned to a new way of thinking. And they willingly move deeper into the life of the group. Adherents are fed a repetitious diet of information, but are consistently deprived of meaningful handles with which to evaluate it. Every cultic circle is its own self-contained system that incrementally seals his membership from a larger world of religious ideas. It is always a fortress mentality.

Cultic Groups Push a Total-Immersion Lifestyle

The busy calendar of social events, endless instruction and training, and other regular group activities keep the faithful engaged. These also curb introspection and re-evaluation, and limit alternatives. Participation is the measure of one's faithfulness and diligence. Instruction is detailed and repetitious, keeping the minds and hearts of adherents continually bathed in the fundamental beliefs and practices of the group. This constant drone of familiar doctrine and rhetoric provides the ongoing conditioning without which the cult could not sustain its influence and control.

Cultic Groups Cultivate a Fear-Hostility Posture to Outsiders

This kind of conditioning is blatantly apparent is some circles, subtle in others, but always present. As members become groomed in a defensive-aggressive stance to outsiders, they are driven even deeper into the life of the cult. The conviction that outsiders are deceived, resistant to God's way and threatening to lead them away from the truth is carefully planted and nurtured. This is a strategy, and by it the faithful are easily isolated and insulated from former associations. This antagonism-fear mechanism prompts a religious reflex, so that when the buttons are pressed, the faithful instinctively switch off their minds and start mouthing carbon copy responses. Surprisingly small doses of paranoia keep the people in the palm of Big Brother's hand.

Cultic Groups Always Reduce the Roles of Jesus

Even when the divine nature and uniqueness of Jesus is professed, the full salvation he brings and his full sufficiency for spiritual life is undermined in various ways. Even as he speaks of the grace of God and the sacrifice of Christ, every cultist knows he must embrace the beliefs and practices of the group, and live within the system if he is to find full acceptance and favor before God. At the for-all-practical-purposes level, keeping oneself in God's good graces has more to do with his participation in the cult than his personal relationship with Jesus. Members are kept in perpetual uneasiness, never quite sure if they have done enough, given enough, or been obedient enough. Assurance is intentionally kept a little beyond their reach and is never a settled question. The dilemma of an insecure relationship with God creates a psychological bondage and keeps the faithful striving and working within the system.

Cultic Groups Double-Talk and Redefine Familiar Terms

Every cultic club has its own insider lingo and vocabulary, often familiar Christian terms than have been injected with new shades and meanings to fit the belief system of the group. Their explanations may sound vaguely familiar and rather convincing, but cloaking the communication with common Christian language creates deepening layers of confusion, which increase the turmoil and unsettledness about one's own beliefs. And, as I read somewhere and scribbled on a note, " . . . into this newly cultivated ground, the foreign seed of their beliefs is systematically planted and watered." A brilliant strategy—first creating the confusing disturbance, then prescribing the remedy!

Cultic Groups Pitch to Spiritual Pride

This is a primary hook. The privilege and honor of being included among the special few or God's chosen ones, and the feeling of being more obedient, more spiritual, and more enlightened than all the others is continually nourished within the cult. Cults not only master the manipulative powers of guilt and shame—and the leverage these emotions hold over people—but they also play with flattery. The clever use of shame and guilt pulls adherents into conformity and submission, but the quiet stroking of pride is itself a powerful motivator. But here is the trade-off: One gains a deepening sense of spiritual superiority, but loses his individuality and interior spiritual freedom in the process. We must never underestimate the power of our own pride as "the tie that binds.'"

Summary Remarks

A cult is a manipulative and exploitative socio-religious structure, regardless of whether its presenting face is a weird religion or a rather orthodox take on Christian faith. Well-managed control is always at the heart of it. Belief structures and tight lines of logic are the means employed to trap the mind into submission and induce compliance. But the baseline agenda is to maintain and extend its power over people. Cults are, at this level, fully preoccupied with controlling someone else's personal and spiritual life.

Emotional triggers are planted, nurtured, and then exploited to induce specific responses and behaviors. Fear is sown through thinly veiled warnings, and insecurities are stimulated by a performance-based culture. Shame and flattery are alternately used, but both with manipulative ends. "Buzzwords" mean little to the outsider, but to the initiated they are emotionally charged, filled with specific content; their simple mention conjures up a full plate of connotations and responses. The dread of displeasing the Lord is carefully managed and effectively used to emotionally manipulate the faithful. Adherents are fully conditioned to believe that jumping off the train means missing out on God's will for them, and a falling out with leadership constitutes a major falling out with the Lord.

Typical for Christians who have emerged from cultic life is to wonder how God would ever let this happen to them. Some have a crisis of faith—some lose faith—and others never fully recover from the deep sense of betrayal and shame. We were party to the process that seduced us and took us in, and we said "yes" at every turn of the road. We felt the prideful glow of being a specially chosen one; we wanted the fast-track to higher spirituality that was offered, and we liked feeling we were closer to God than other ordinary Christians. The thought-stopping techniques we employed to block our own dissenting thoughts and stop all incoming fire against the group undoubtedly blocked many overtures from God's Spirit. We unwittingly resisted his prompts to think for ourselves and to see the contradictions before us. As we were fighting off everybody and everything else, we were pushing him away too. And this is but one part of a full baggage car that every former member of a cult has before him. I am convinced there are few who have quickly rolled over and gotten back up on their feet.

Within any cult structure and any cult member, there is always an inherent dishonesty and elitism at the core. We might perceive this as a persistent disturbing vibe, the feeling that something is just not right, when we are around such people. But that intuition will only diminish as we permit ourselves to become acclimatized and rationalized toward it. It is important to read it as spiritual discernment, God's voice to us, and a warning to be acted upon. We need to go away and keep our distance because none of us possesses natural immunity from manipulative spiritual enticement. The human mind is not as strong as we think it is, and there is too much going on here for any of us to handle in isolation.

Chapter Ten

The Manifest Sons of God Doctrine:
The Phantom in the Opera

Constitutional to the New Order of the Latter Rain which emerged in the late 1940s was the "Manifestation of the Sons of God" motif. "Phantom" is not an unfair descriptor because for many decades it was handled as insider knowledge not to be recklessly disclosed to an unreceptive and unbelieving Christian world. Within a few years, the Latter Rain movement was of little consequence to mainline Pentecostal denominations, but their ministries remained active on the periphery, travelling internationally and widely impacting independent Pentecostal groups with their prolific writing and publishing. And this anchor doctrine was at the heart of their message.

The early Charismatic movement afforded wide-open expanses, but beyond the identifiable camps, the Manifest Sons of God doctrine was largely underground and quietly peddled on the fringes. From time to time one would see pop-ups: an ambiguous remark suggesting something else but no further comment, a hint without being forthright, and something never laid on the table for examination and evaluation. A very insecure person once told me he thought I must be a true son of God but he did not believe he could ever become one. I knew immediately where this came from and was appalled at how this sad man had no idea of who he was in Christ. The essential doctrine has persisted, and moved from its original keepers through diverse circles to contemporary proponents. Still, whenever I hear key words and defining phrases, I never know for certain how much of the full package has been embraced.

The theology remains controversial on several fronts. For starters, it presents itself as the future hope of the true church against the entrenched Pre-tribulation Rapture position. The Rapture theory is flatly dismissed as a false hope. Secondly, the Manifest Sons of God doctrine undergirds some "dominion" theologies of the Charismatic genre, which envision the true church extending its spiritual and political authority, and subduing the whole earth before Christ returns. Thirdly, the teaching crosses accepted Christian beliefs by redefining "sonship" in progressive levels of maturity, eliminating everyone but an elite spiritual circle from the coveted status of "true" sons of God. These alone will be gloriously manifested as the very image of Christ, his incarnation on earth and essentially his second coming. And a veiled inference of this special company being transformed into divine beings never fades away completely because it is neither clearly confirmed nor categorically denied. "Slinky" is the descriptive word. The Manifest Sons of God doctrine has long been the phantom in the opera, stirring the waters, then melding into the shadows.

The Spiritualizing Undercarriage that Carries the Doctrine

The Latter Rain movement was the fountainhead from which most of the spiritualizing modes in the Charismatic movement derive. A firm conviction that deeper spiritual realities lie beneath the literal "letter" of the Scriptures is pervasive in all their theological thought, and overrides everything else. George Warnock's *The Feast of Tabernacles: The Hope of the Church* is probably the clearest representation of classic Latter Rain theology. The book in its entirely is a multi-faceted biblical allegory of what they aspired to be and their hoped-for destiny in these last days. The goal was their glorious transformation into an invincible army of the Lord which would establish Christ's Kingdom over the entire world. The historical tensions between themselves and classical Pentecostals are in the immediate backdrop. The classic Pentecostal never moved beyond the Feast of Pentecost and essentially remains in a spiritual dark age, but they esteemed themselves the recipients of the new revelation and moving toward the fulfillment of the Feast of Tabernacles.

The spiritualizing does not begin in the pages of the Bible. The actual starting point was assumptions they held about themselves and the role they looked for in God's final work on earth. Interpretation, for them, was putting their already well-defined theology and hopes for themselves into the story lines, the religious observances and the symbols in the Bible. And in the process, they overlaid a vast array of biblical passages with incredibly elitist depictions of themselves.

Latter Rain attitudes and reactions to Christian believers beyond their borders were between dismissive and contemptuous in the literature, although some later tracts moderated the vitriol. I have been surprised to see in actual life and practice how well some have transcended the condescension. The Rapture of the Church in the Pre-tribulation paradigm was the antithesis of Latter Rain views, and much criticism was directed at carnal, earthly minded believers who subscribed to it. History and experience also had some bearing on their general posture. Immediately preceding the Latter Rain revival of 1948, a falling out between two instructors at the denominational Bible school and the Saskatchewan district of the Pentecostal Assemblies of Canada created a rift. Seventy students from the school followed George Hawtin and Percy Hunt to Sharon Bible School in North Battleford. Almost predictably, mainline Pentecostalism is given much unflattering press in Latter Rain allegorical interpretation. It is the foil, the straw man in the story line—and has been ever since.

One experiences on occasion the strange sensation of hearing the familiar promises of Scripture but intuitively knowing that they are not being included by the one speaking of them. This is typical of Latter Rain literature and preaching, and successors to their tradition. And it is true—one is not being included in the greatest of God's promises simply by virtue of being a born-again believer and pursuing Christ. Proponents regard them as promises that apply quite exclusively to themselves because the Christian church at large has forfeited them, having neither heard them nor responded to them over the centuries. They see themselves the "faithful remnant," the true heirs of all those good promises from God, and read the Scriptures through those eyeglasses. Thus, they easily see themselves as the "new temple" that God is building even though the original passage in Ephesians speaks to all who are in Christ. Protestant and evangelical faiths of all kinds are regarded as desolate and spiritually barren, and the greatest of God's promises no longer apply to them. Hence, the Latter Rain and their successors quite comfortably deem themselves on the fast track to becoming the true bride of Christ, the Church within the Church, and in pole position for becoming the true sons of God. They were, after all, the enlightened ones who believed the message.

Unmasking the Spiritual Gaming in "Spiritualizing"

A precedent for comprehensive spiritual interpretation, Latter Rain proponents would point out, is right there in the New Testament use of the Jewish scriptures. Old Testament types, prophecies, and statements specifically addressed to national Israel are carried forward into the New Covenant and given a new mold, a distinctively Christian application. They have been recast in terms of the new people of God and the new spiritual Israel. Both Jews and Gentiles comprise the one new man in Christ.

I concur this is precisely what New Testament authors are doing at numerous points, and their message is clear: Redemptive history rolls forward to its spiritual fulfillment in Jesus and issues in one new people of God, who are heirs to many promises given under the former covenant. But contemporary allegorists are deviating and distorting the picture when they insist they are doing the same thing. They are not.

The founding apostolic ministries were laying the very foundation of the long-prophesied New Covenant, a baseline that was comprehensive, inclusive and cosmic in scope—and anchored at every point to Jesus Christ himself. They were the apostolic generation who were called by Jesus himself to set the essential demarcations of what was carried forward, what was left behind, and what was adapted to fit the new order. That foundational task was completed, and everything else has been a building upon that foundation of Jesus Christ—for the better or for the worse.

Much of the subsequent spiritualizing interpretation which presumes to pick up the apostolic task and carry it forward has been for the worse. It invariably narrows the scope of God's great purposes to hinge upon ourselves and whatever movement we are party to. Christ remains the figurehead but we become the main players now. We create our own allegorical production by staging ourselves at the center of God's great drama and writing our own scripts into salvation history—and crossing out the lines of all who disagree with us. We give them bit parts and use them as foils to enlarge our image of ourselves. This is "building" upon the foundation of Christ that has been laid? No, this is demolition. This is vintage sectarian Pentecostalism.

Paul's analogy of Hagar and Sarah in Galatians 4:22–31 would have been perfect material for Pentecostal-Charismatic allegorizing, and the Latter Rain folk would not have missed it— had not the apostle Paul claimed it first. He applied it to contrast those who have faith in Christ to those living under the Old Covenant. The first son was born under the old Sinai covenant, the child of the slave woman, disinherited and a citizen of an earthly Jerusalem that is itself in slavery and persecuting the true heir. The other son was born of a free woman under a new covenant, the child of a promise, born of the power of the Spirit and a citizen of a heavenly city. Paul's point is clear: Do not go back to reclaim old baggage that has no claim on you, and no part in the inheritance God has given us in Christ. And those born of the power of the Spirit must stand firm in that freedom because it is their inheritance.

This is the perfect "dualistic" picture with all the components for creative spiritualizing: the new and the old, the good and the bad, the spiritual and the unspiritual, the heavenly and the earthly, and the persecuted and the persecutor. The Pentecostal-Charismatic allegorist would have immediately identified himself with the new, the good, the spiritual, the heavenly, and the persecuted. He would then have scanned the horizon and put the crosshairs on his cousins with whom he has ongoing hostilities. He would see them fitting the dark side of the analogy so perfectly, and properly belonging with the unbelieving and earthly minded masses of Christendom. How absurd is this? Yet this is precisely what the Latter Rain movement in general and George Warnock in particular—and all successors—have consistently done and continue to do with their "spiritualizing" theologies. The process is petty, sectarian, and stuffed with untruths. And the product is base, self-righteous, and prideful. There is nothing of the transcendence, the cosmic proportion, and the Christ-centeredness that we find in the New Testament writers' use of the Old Testament. The end result, I suggest, sheds more light on the baser human element than it does on some hidden "truth" in Scripture.

Unmasking the Phantom in the Opera

The Manifest Sons of God doctrine was core to a disclosure of hidden spiritual knowledge to those gathered for prayer and fasting at North Battleford, Saskatchewan in the spring of 1948. The message was that God was *beginning* his great restoration of all that has been lost in the fall of the church and the fall of Adam, that he was going to bring deliverance and restoration to his creation. And he would do this by removing the veil and initiating his people into the mysteries of God. This was radically "realized" eschatology, with the faithful maturing toward their fullness in Christ under the essential fivefold ministry offices and ideally culminating in their full manifestation as "sons" of God. They were "now at this time" front and center at this most crucial juncture in salvation history, and on the brink of God's restoration of all things.

And other Christian believers? If they believed and received the message, they too would be incorporated into this great work of God. If not, they still would eat the manna from heaven and drink the water from the rock, yet they would die in the wilderness and never see this inheritance from the Lord. Evangelicals in general were dismissed as too Laodicean, and other Pentecostals fared no better. Though they had been blessed and provided for in their wilderness wanderings for the last forty years or so (since the early 1900s birth of the Pentecostal movement), they too were of that generation that refused to cross the border into Canaan. Hence, the Latter Rain "message" became its own gospel dividing those who believe God from those who refuse him—a device which finds no end of usefulness in the Pentecostal-Charismatic world. It is the same old Pentecostal scramble to see who is most spiritual among us all and closest to God.

My wife and I have had for many years a friendly connection with a senior Latter Rain couple who have been with the movement from the earliest years. He functioned in a "ministry" and for decades travelled internationally. In an after-supper conversation she mentioned she was troubled by the prospect of not recognizing her husband in eternity. I was puzzled by her concern, and my little spiel about "being glorified yet still being ourselves," from the exchange of glances between them, told me I had missed it by a mile. But it came to me. In the warmth of fellowship I had forgotten we were different brands of Pentecostal and I had forgotten some of the finer points of their life-to-come doctrine. Only God knows whom he has predestined to full sonship. She was concerned that her husband might be found sufficiently faithful, but she might not. And, if so, his incredible transformation into the very image of Christ as one of the Manifest Sons of God might render him completely unrecognizable to her.

The banner verse of this doctrine, of course, derives from Paul's letter to the Christian church in Rome:

> The creation waits in eager expectation for the sons of God to be revealed. For the creation was subjected to frustration, not by its own choice, but by the will of him who subjected it, in hope that the creation itself will be liberated from its bondage to decay and brought into the glorious freedom of the children of God. (Romans 8:19–21).

Christian believers in general read here the resurrection of their bodies, the decisive freedom from death and decay, and the transforming glorification Christ will bring to his creation at the end of the age. They do so because they believe they have become God's children through faith in Christ. Manifest Sons of God doctrine, however, recasts "sonship" in tiers of spiritual maturity and worthiness, and only a select faithful company of themselves are predestined to full sonship. Only God, through his foreknowledge of their faithfulness, knows who they are. One becomes a child of God by believing; one becomes a son by obedience. It is the combination of basic salvation and personal progress that leads one toward full sonship, and the prescribed fivefold ministries claim to lay the path.

These will be the "sons of God," described in Romans chapter 8 and it is they, gloriously transfigured and divinely empowered, who will be Christ's second coming to earth. Jesus will indeed return, but *after* they have conquered the kingdoms of this world for him.

In the literature, the physical coming of Jesus is consistently pale and anti-climactic compared to his incarnational accomplishments in the overcoming sons of God. They will proclaim a worldwide gospel and perform great miracles, transcending the coming Tribulation and fulfilling the works of God. All others will be part of the great falling away which will have already come to pass. These true sons of God, immortal incarnations of Christ in their glorious manifestation and ministry, will be physically visible yet untouchable and invulnerable. Warnock was colorful in his depictions, investing this overcoming company with powers to appear and disappear, and to call down manna from heaven. He presents them immune to hot and cold, and unscathed by nuclear weaponry. Later writers tone down their descriptions of "Joel's army." These are they, it is claimed, who, having subdued the political and spiritual kingdoms of this world, will rule and reign with Christ. Collectively, they are the "man-child" of Revelation 12:5, who was snatched up to God and to his throne. They are the "one" destined to rule all the nations of the earth with an iron sceptre.

The Persistent Haziness Surrounding Full "Sonship"

Ambiguity has always surrounded the notion of full "sonship" and never receives real clarification. Occasionally someone, like a kid with no discretion about family business and who thinks he knows everything, cannot wait to tell it all and blurts out, "We are gods." It is untraceable of course, but one knows they did not just pick it up themselves from Jesus' response to the Jews in John 10:34–35 and Peter's words about "participating in the divine nature" (2 Peter 1:4). I assume the recurrent duplicity of speech is intentional.

In short, I believe a conflation of the believer's *glorification* and a notion of *divinization* is being played with just beneath the surface of the conversation. Warnock in his treatise comes close without exactly saying it. In the unveiling of the true sons of God, they will be "made exactly like him" and "transfigured into the same image" (with his emphasis on "same"). "The overcomer will live the very same life as the only begotten Son of God" (p.115). The inference is sown, then left to float at the level of implication.

All Christians should have some notion of being little incarnations of Christ, but the Latter Rain and later adherents of the doctrine are not playing with the metaphor. The "manifestation of the sons of God" is loaded terminology. It is the defining revelation and glorification of the overcoming company of true sons. This is the spiritual second coming of Christ, the manifestation of "the Son," the manifestation of the Christ in them (Hinchcliff, 1999:35). Christ was incarnate in one man—Jesus—in his first coming. In his return at the end of the age, he will be incarnate in the "many-membered man-child," the elect sons that God will bring forth out of the church and will transfigure into the very image of Christ.

The equivocation, the double meaning, can be shifted one way or the other. The dealer can play the card as he chooses. Look at it in one shade and it suggests a variation of the Mormon's journey to divinity. Look at it again and it appears not that far from something one might already believe. This is the "phantom" that appears, then slips out of reach just as quickly—and this too is part of the opera.

Chapter Eleven

Camp on the Highest Hill:
Our Spiritual "Add-Ons" are a Minus for Christ

The highest hill gives the best vantage point to read the lay of the land. Plant your feet firmly on the New Testament revelation, of which you are a living participant, and that will give you the best view of the entire Bible. The common mistake is to view the Scriptures as one large, level playing field, when in fact God's revelation of himself and his salvation keeps ascending as it moves through human history, and reaches its pinnacle in Jesus Christ.

All Scripture is divinely inspired ("God-breathed") but all is not of equal importance to us. It took many long centuries of moving onwards and upwards for the full picture to come into view. Two well-defined covenant relationships are in view, and though the New Covenant builds on the former, it also fulfils and supplants it. From early in the book of Genesis, we easily see God moving through the Scriptures and through the centuries with a progressively unfolding disclosure of himself and his saving purposes. The story line proceeds with increasing fullness and clarity until it culminates in the coming of Jesus, God's own Son, to inaugurate a New Covenant built upon himself.

The implications are obvious: our final, verifying word on matters of faith and practice should be derived from the New Testament, not the Old. The decisive word on Christian doctrine must be confirmed in the very Scriptures that embody, clarify and specify the New Covenant relationship under which we live. Particulars and practices from the Old Testament do not automatically transfer into the New. Some are carried forward and added to; some are ignored and phased out; some are internalized; and some are universalized. Some functions, like the former priesthood, temple and sacrificial system were completely fulfilled in Christ and are now obsolete. The New Testament, and particularly the apostolic revelation in the epistles, gives us filters and lenses for looking at the Old Testament. We need to use them. We do not get closer to Jesus by going backwards.

Ignoring the progressive nature of God's revelation, and squeezing the new wine of Christian faith into the old wineskins and forms of Judaism, reverses the flow, producing confusion and bad theology. Circles that establish their distinctives—those doctrines which define and set them apart—from the Jewish Scriptures, are scanning the Bible as if it were equally weighty and relevant at both ends. And so, Old Testament dietary regulations, the traditional Sabbath observance, and playing God's Old Covenant name against the New Covenant name of Jesus, become hills to die on.

The intrigue some believers have with Jewish religious motifs and observances is their personal interest and freedom. It is a cultural embellishment of their choosing. But these become an issue whenever they are promoted as an "ought" or a ticket to true spiritual enrichment. Preaching the gospel and planting churches in the larger world of the Mediterranean regions, the apostle Paul and company faced opposition from three fronts: the idolatrous Gentile social order under Rome, hostile Jewish synagogues, and Jewish Christians who were insistent that Gentile Christian converts needed to be circumcised and follow the Law of Moses too. The continual clash Paul and his associates had with these Christian

"Judaizers" gave rise to many New Testament passages that settle on this one thing: none of us is going to become a better Christian by becoming a better Jew. And none of us is going to become a better Christian with a whole assortment of other "add-ons" either.

Beware of "Jesus-Plus-Something-Else" Religion

Someone coined the expression "Jesus Plus" religion to speak of the spiritual add-ons we use to set ourselves apart from other Christian believers or add our own terms to God's plan of salvation. The irony is that our "additions" always end up as a "minus" for Christ. We imagine they give us something deeper, but they always give us something less.

Under the Old Covenant order, people of Israelite stock and adherents to Jewish faith were uniquely the people of God. Indeed, Jewish faith was both the light of the world and the door to the sheepfold. So the coming of Christ brought some particularly good news to the God-fearing outsider because he no longer needed to become a Jew in order to come to God. And there would be no necessity or benefit for him to act like one afterwards. He simply had to come to Christ—and Christ alone.

The gospel of Jesus Christ does an end run around Judaism's corner on God and gives everyone direct, immediate access to God through Jesus himself. This point, interestingly enough, was more immediately offensive to Jewish sensibilities than the claim that Jesus was the Messiah and the risen Son of God. Previously, the Jews alone were regarded as "Abraham's seed" and heirs of the promises spoken to Abraham. Gentiles (non-Jews) entered the realm of God's full blessing through the rite of circumcision. But the apostle Paul establishes that Christ himself is "Abraham's seed" (Galatians 3:16) and non-Jewish peoples are fully accepted and enter into the full blessing of Abraham in the New Covenant through the blood of Christ alone.

The earliest Christians were completely and deeply Jewish, and struggled long and hard to sort out their relationship to the Law of Moses and the Gentiles. It appears few Judean Christian believers transcended their religious ethnocentric heritage and fully embraced the scope and vision of the New Testament message. It was the Hellenistic believers in the cities around the Mediterranean, those deeply immersed in Greek culture, who embraced the gospel for the whole world and really ran with it. The apostle Paul and the Christian churches he established were continually harassed by Jewish-Christians who relentlessly propagated their "Jesus Plus the Law of Moses" campaign among the churches in the Mediterranean territories.

More than once my wife has told me if she met Paul the apostle she probably would not like him, that he seems arrogant to her. I do not know, I have never met him. But I like him a lot. I like him because he and his fellow workers stood their ground, and because of that a worldwide vision for the Gospel was planted in those regions. I cannot imagine James the brother of the Lord receiving the clarity and I cannot envision Peter having the courage to withstand this powerful Jewish-Christian wall. The simplicity of the gospel was saved and I am a direct beneficiary of that. I enjoy it to the fullest and I have the highest regard for Paul and his associates.

New Covenant teaching draws an explicit line on these issues. The coming of Jesus annuls the old division between Jew and Gentile because an experience in Christ makes "one new man" out of them both (Ephesians 2:14–16). "Circumcision of the heart" is what makes both Jew and Gentile the people of God in this age. The New Testament Scriptures refute any necessity or advantage, and display no interest in the rite of circumcision and the observance of prescribed holy days from the old order. It regards them as shadowy images of what was to come, but the reality of those things is only found in Jesus Christ himself (Colossians 2:16–17). All the treasures of wisdom and knowledge are hidden in him and only him (Colossians 2:3).

Don't Let People Bring You into Bondage:
Insights from Paul's Letter to the Galatians

"Don't let people bring you into bondage." A former Bible college president said those words on more than one occasion. And they have come to mind many times in the passing decades. We Pentecostal-Charismatics should not have to gaze too deeply to see a reflection of ourselves in the troubled waters of the Galatian churches. When they only had their faith in Jesus Christ and God's Holy Spirit in them, they really did have it all. But in their immaturity, they could neither see it nor leave it at that. Consequently, they were enticed by claims of a more complete light in the Law of Moses. That is us! Like them, having begun in the Spirit, we too are seduced by man-made spiritual add-ons like prescribed requirements, esoteric knowledge, revelatory claims and invitations to link arms with God's band of empowered and enlightened super-Christians. We eat this up! Having begun in the Spirit, we too are easily derailed by false teachings and human designs. This is our Achilles heel.

The methodology then was the same as today. The Galatian believers were running well, until certain legalistic Jewish Christians did their own intervention. Paul asks them, "Who cut in on you and kept you from obeying the truth?" (5:7). Not everyone sees our freedom in Christ as a wonderful thing or respects it. Spiritual opportunists cannot leave it alone. Paul tells them in the next verse that this kind of persuasion, despite its claims, does not come from God. False teaching and those who peddle it always come with the same agenda, namely, a scheme to extend their sphere of personal influence over people's lives: "These people are zealous to win you over, but for no good" (4:17a).

And their strategy is just as predictable: "What they want is to alienate you [from us] so that you may be zealous for them" (4:17b). Fishing for disciples, errorists of all flavors divide and conquer by separating persons from their beliefs and frames of reference, alienating them from their faith associations and roots of fellowship, and drawing them away after themselves. They make a good impression outwardly (6:12).

Paul asks a pertinent question: "What has happened to all your joy?" (4:15) The subtle departure of our joy is an early indicator we are into something of a man-made religious nature and feeling the weight of a burden we did not carry before. I am not speaking of the exuberance we feel in the heat of collective worship; I am referring to the quiet joy in our hearts when we are completely alone. This is the first thing to go. Those, having begun in the Spirit, do not always finish that way. Misled by promises of a spiritual fast-track to power, enlightenment, and leadership, some are seduced and unwittingly abandon their freedom and joy in Christ. They trade away authentic life and spiritual freedom and turn back to the basic religious principles of this world (4:9).

The Devious Game in "Deeper Truth:"
Insights from Paul's Letter to the Colossians

The letter to the Colossians, especially the first two chapters, is not an easy read. Still, it remains a treasury of memorable verses and particularly bold statements about Jesus the divine Son of God. There is, however, a particular church problem here—not overwhelming perhaps, but "incipient," that is, becoming apparent and needing to be addressed. As we pick up the flow of thought, we glimpse the faces of error working on the fringes of the Colossian church. And if we are perceptive, we see the same parade of superior wisdom and enlightenment (Colossians 2:8), subscription to prescribed religious regulations (2:16–17, 20–23), and inflated claims of revelatory spiritual experiences (2:18–19) that is played out in our contemporary Pentecostal-Charismatic world.

Error, then and now, whether embedded in full-blown cults or carried in home-spun heresies, or peddled in Christian fads, is always a deviation and distraction from the centrality and supremacy of Jesus Christ. Error is cleverly packaged and cleverly solicited. It is always couched in a compelling opportunity to be among God's elite, to be chosen from among the many, and to join the crème de la crème. Falsehoods target our spiritual aspirations and gently stroke our pride. They promise quick tickets to true enlightenment and intimate proximity to God. Error plays to the secret elitism in our hearts and invariably sets us up for a significant derailment from Christ-centered faith.

"Disqualification" is essential to this game. One's Christian life as it stands must be depreciated and discredited, so they will see proponents of the new light as superior, and aspire to be like them. One's faith in Christ alone must be undercut, so that one will defer to them, and they might extend their sphere of influence and jurisdiction over them. Purveyors of error make a hard sell, and it is not surprising that the apostle Paul expressly states in his opening statements that God himself "has *qualified* us to share in the inheritance of the saints" (1:12). And later, he instructs his readers not to let those who revel in ascetic practices, or preoccupy themselves with angels and visions, "*disqualify* you for the prize" (2:18). Do not accept their judgment on you, he says. Such persons are puffed up with idle notions and have lost connection with Christ who is the Head of the body (2:18–19). The point is clear: If God has fully *qualified* you in and through Christ, do not let men *disqualify* you with their deceptive and misleading schemes.

So why does Paul extol the greatness and supremacy of Christ at such length and in such depth in his letter to these Christians? Precisely to convince the reader of Christ's absolute sufficiency and supremacy in all things, and to undercut the earthbound religiosities of mere men that keep creeping in from the sidelines. If all the treasures of wisdom and knowledge are hidden in Christ (2:3)—and we have a direct and living connection to him—then what is a merely human philosophy going to do for us? What is the wisdom of this world and even its most plausible arguments, or even a religious tradition, going to add to our life in Christ? What are religious dietary regulations, annual Jewish festivals, monthly celebrations, and allotted Sabbath days (2:16–17) to us, except shadows and pointers from the past?

Spiritual reality is only in Christ himself and we are already in him! And if all the fullness of God dwells in Christ (2:9), and we "have been given fullness in Christ, who is the head over every power and authority" (2:10), then what are religious displays of humility, particular supernatural experiences and visions, and obsessions with angelic beings going to add to our faith—except more distraction from Christ himself? And what are human commands and taboos, and man-made ordinances going to accomplish for us? They look wise; they look spiritual and they look worshipful, but they are impotent to restrain our self-indulgent human natures (2:20–23) because there is no divine life and no power of God in them.

None of us is beyond admonition and correction. We must regard the spiritual authorities who are over us in the Lord and submit ourselves to their leadership. Still, no person has a direct claim on our lives or mediates our access to God and his graces except Jesus Christ himself and Jesus Christ alone. And Jesus does not farm us out to spiritual subcontractors.

Error comes with a claw that makes us subservient to those who will prescribe for us what to think, what to do and what to believe— and sever us from the reality of being personally led by the Spirit. Don't let people bring you into bondage. Do not let anyone insinuate themselves into your inner spiritual spaces, gaining leverage for themselves with their seductive logic and grandiose claims. When (if) you come to your senses, you will feel outrageously violated, and you will be tormented with the realization that you willingly conceded to every step of your journey into error.

The familiar Charismatic chime of "God is doing a new thing" has often enough borne, just beneath the surface, yet another new religiosity or recycled an old one. It captures the limelight for a time before drifting to the periphery or going underground for a season. The real criterion of Christian "truth" is not how tidily we have bundled it up or how popular our interpretations of our spiritual experiences have become. Rather, truth has everything to do with what we have done with the centrality and the absolute supremacy of Jesus Christ in the process.

Is the vision and role of Jesus himself enlarged in the eyes of the believer, or is Jesus diminished and the human component enlarged and glorified instead? Are we lifting up ourselves and our structures to heavenly heights, or are we lifting up Christ? Are we glorifying him, or are we pumping up human leadership? The presentation of Jesus Christ in Colossians is overwhelmingly large and majestic—deliberately so, to blow away the man-made competition on the fringes, and the "Jesus Plus" religion they are peddling. So I will stick with the Jesus-Front-and-Center faith that the Scriptures so boldly endorse here.

Parting Remarks

What purports to give us more than Christ leaves us with less of him. How does one add anything to his "fullness?" Elitist Pentecostal-Charismatic packages take no one deeper in Christ. They are a dilution and never an authentic avenue to a deeper Christian spirituality because they are just us injecting ourselves and our human religiosities (the basic principles of this world) into spaces that only Jesus Christ can fill. Christ, and he alone, fills the vast expanse between the highest heaven and ourselves. The gap is neither filled with a string of spiritual emanations, as certain Gnostics thought, nor a line of mediating human ministries, as many Charismatics think. Jesus himself is the "one mediator between God and men" (1 Tim. 2:5) and needs no secondary, little "Christs" standing between himself and the Christian believer.

Most of us, especially this generation, are wary of "legalisms" but are not so alert to claims of directive revelations from God. We must shake off the claw of so-called higher spiritual knowledge that imposes its own will on its adherents. Each of these assails the all-sufficiency of Christ that he himself mediates to the believer. Each of these affords an opportunity to the human element and darker spiritual entities to do their own interventions in a believer's life. And if neither legalistic observances nor esoteric knowledge and supernatural experiences can overcome our lower impulses, how then are they going to take us to a higher Christian spirituality? Everything is already there in Jesus Christ, and in him alone.

This is the apostolic foundation Paul is laying down. Are we going to overlay this with another apostolic baseline of our own?

Closing

The Cult of Leadership
. . . and the Insatiable Thirst for Spiritual Leverage

"Submission and Authority," I am sure, is past finding consensus in Pentecostal domains, and will ever be unfinished business. Leadership and good church management is about control, the right kind of control and oversight. We are called in Scripture to submit ourselves to those in leadership because they are called to do the leading and we are not. And we need a structure so that those given the responsibility of leading have the appropriate autonomy and space to do it. Most everyone acknowledges these principles in general but from there it diverges. The debate is layered in justifying rationales and well beyond an honest conversation.

Fifty or sixty years ago, church authority and submission had the women in its sights, and among biblical literalists, the discussion boxed the women in with head coverings, not speaking aloud in church, and not instructing the men—and not being ordained. In church culture, the husband's authority and his wife's corresponding submission was a live item. Roles for husbands and wives were clearly marked out in the larger culture. When Grandpa wanted to bolster his authority in the home he would point to the prescribed roles of men and women as divine givens, add the "Wives, submit" passages and become very legal and self-righteous. Passages about husbands loving their wives, obviously given to qualify and give a context for any submission he might be expecting, were invisible to him. But over time, roles of men and women changed drastically in the larger culture, the church, and the home. Roles and expectations have become more negotiable and less defined, and the constant heat of the old debate has dissipated in most sectors.

The submission and authority issue among Pentecostal-Charismatics is where the man and woman debate was decades ago. Church leadership roles and corresponding roles of average believers quickly became well defined (and sometimes over defined) against the backdrop of an amorphous, turbulent, prophetically-driven people movement. The five ministry categories in Paul's letter to the Ephesians were carefully combed over and filled with very specific content, content which had and still has immediate implications on the question of submission to leadership. The "submission" side of the equation was quickly filled with new content too, with average believers being made to understand just what was expected from them.

Just how biblical is the "content" part of the debate? Well, certainly as biblical as Grandpa's relationship to Grandma was, but in retrospect we see how tracked and self-interested that was. Paul's church letters and the letter to the Hebrews (evidently from someone in Paul's circle) display a consistency in their formats: thick theological discussions giving way to practical concerns, then finally breaking into compact, often one-liner exhortations and instructions, a few greetings and then the closing. Submission to spiritual-authority exhortations in the New Testament are usually of the middle abbreviated, general category, like "Obey your leaders and submit to their authority. They keep watch over you as men who must give an account. Obey them so that their work will be a joy . . ." (Hebrews 13:17).

Who works out the scope of applications for verses such as this in a Charismatic world—the rank and file to whom the passage is addressed, or just their leaders? And how should that be done? Simply by fiat? The few submission-to-authority passages we have are bare boned. Where did all the content come from that we have poured into them over the last forty years? The short answer is from our own Pentecostal-Charismatic culture, our hastily assembled traditions, and our own deductions about spiritual leadership, just like Grandpa got the big chunk of his content from his larger social world, his church culture, and his own personal assumptions. Neither Grandpa nor ourselves had as much *biblical content* as we presumed.

We probably had some wisdom from the Holy Spirit at some points in the journey, but even that was obscured as some tried to upscale the whole program with less-than-convincing "revelations" of their own. My point is this: little of the content in the Charismatic submission and authority models is directly sourced from God at all, and beyond the general principle, little of it is inherently biblical. The large blanket of applications has been our doing, and to this day comparatively autonomous leadership extends that blanket to reach wherever they want it to go. They keep adding to it with their own deductive logic. Beneath the spiritual spin and the mirrors, it is essentially and obviously very human theology.

The Shepherding movement within a few short years took "submission" over the edge in many churches. Within the circle, the problem was generally attributed to bad pastoral practice and not the theology. This is a mistake: it was bad pastoral practice that had been legitimized by flawed assumptions about pastoral jurisdiction over people's lives. The "theology" had been formulated by that very generation of leaders to sanction the kind of authority, the spiritual hierarchy, and the spheres of control they wanted. Those who borrowed the models were top-level authorities in their own assemblies, and the shepherding structure endorsed the blanket authority and level of personal autonomy they wished to maintain. They shaped the specific discipleship-accountability philosophies for their own use, gave them their own "God stamp," and imposed them on their assemblies. They convinced their people that it was all from God. No one was innocent of the abuse that ensued.

Little has changed at a fundamental level in contemporary shepherding circles. The former shepherding-discipleship motif, because of the negative association, has been given new names and new clothes, sweetened up some, but still runs on the same old tracks. The contemporary overseer is more approachable, more fatherly and mentoring, and less a "church boss" in his presentation. But the underlying footings are the same. Many elements in contemporary submission-authority fellowships track back to prominent Latter Rain themes. The current spiritual father/spiritual sonship paradigms and personal apostle relationships carry forward their essential DNA from earlier ideas of protective spiritual coverings, personal pastors, lifelong discipleship relationships, and tithing to the shepherds. The old hierarchical pyramid once filled with ladders of shepherds and sheep is being supplanted with tiers of spiritual fathers and sons. And on the inside, "submission" remains the operative word.

Though the air has been freshened up, two decades of magnifying the apostolic and prophetic offices have left the baseline even more authoritarian in structure. Apostolic claims keep rising to new heights with correspondingly more dependency, less autonomy, and more submissive posturing on the parts of those under their jurisdiction. The transition from apostles as the top-line spiritual leaders to virtual priests and spiritual intermediaries, dispensing gifts and graces of God, and standing between the believer and Jesus, should raise alarms throughout the Pentecostal-Charismatic world. Charismatics who have been conditioned to believe they cannot advance in their relationship with God apart from a relationship with a personal apostle have been systematically boxed in. They are trapped in a spiral of ongoing personal submission to human leaders, convinced they can only go deeper in God by going deeper with their human handlers.

Limits to spiritual authority, as in bygone days, do not come up for open discussion. Nor does the incredible personal autonomy God has given to each individual believer in Christ, nor the fact that he has implanted his personal presence in their spirit for the express purpose of leading and empowering them. A spokesperson for the current apostolic restoration in a recent magazine article expressed his amazement at how much spiritual authority God was investing in individual leaders these days. This begs the more fundamental question of *whether* God is bestowing that much spiritual authority in them at all. More amazing to me is how much more personal power such personalities can keep ascribing to themselves, and blatantly continue preaching and projecting themselves to the center of everything God is doing.

The "Mindless" Part in the Charismatic Mind

There is a characteristic "mindless" component in the general Charismatic mindset. The great myth seeping through Pentecostal-Charismatic culture, and embraced by many, is that their "theologies" are God's work. These are understood to be something given to their leaders as rather complete packages of truth for the times. Too many are looking for something to simply believe in, to trust completely, to assure themselves of God's will, and to feel a cut above the rest. In this world, such persons are beyond number and there is continually a crop to be harvested. They remain perennially vulnerable because they neither thoughtfully evaluate nor take responsibility for their Christian lives.

What is "theology?" It is essentially a very human endeavor. Even for the zealous Pentecostal-Charismatic variety, the best of it is well-informed by Scripture with some aspects illuminated by the Holy Spirit, but it is still mostly us shaping and articulating our beliefs. It is us assembling our rationales. We do well to realize that anything we devise is, even at its pinnacle, a mix of divine and human energies, never as "biblical"' as we envision it and never as straight-from-God as we like to pitch it. As soon as we begin to analyze and organize what the Scriptures are saying, we are in subtle ways and to considerable measure accommodating them to our way of reasoning. We are filtering them through our own biases and assumptions. The simple truth is we touch it and we taint it. And when we add the spiritual spin to transform it into more of a God thing than it is, we are telling a lie.

The human component in our beliefs, in itself, is not an overwhelming problem. God's Spirit is quite adept at moving "incarnationally" within our imperfect human natures in numerous ways. The dynamics in the operation of a spiritual gift is a case in point. The serious problem comes with the very human temptation to take what is for the most part a human endeavor—like our spiritual traditions or our innovative theological thinking—and artificially exalt them to the status of revelations from God. We then impose them on the people of God by means of misappropriated spiritual authority. This is common fare in Pentecostal-Charismatic territories.

Ministering "Clean"

Our gift, or our particular gift package, is what gives us a platform for an eternal contribution to God's Kingdom and people's lives. We must work on our gifts because they are our primary avenues and contact points for effective spiritual ministry. They are also the "something" in us by which people are drawn to us, as they see a strength in us they know they do not have. Our giftings give us a discernable measure of spiritual authority to which many will defer and almost unconsciously posture themselves to accept our influence and counsel.

Personally-disinterested ministry is essential as this juncture. Integrity and selflessness is crucial because it is at this point that both the opportunity and the temptation arise to attract interest to ourselves. There is a time to step into people's lives for moments of intimate personal ministry and there is a time to get out. When a needy person is too patronizing and too admiring of us, it remains for us to be the big person. We need to step back. Sometimes we must flatten someone's excessive intrigue with our abilities and spiritual gifts.

My wife and I long ago agreed that we would not use our personal ministries to intrude into people's private spaces, that we would always respect a dimension in their persons that belongs exclusively to themselves and God's Holy Spirit in them. We have had at different times spiritual oversight over others, but we have never read that as a jurisdiction over their personal spiritual lives. Only God has that. For us that meant bringing matters right up to their faces, but it remained for them to reach out and take it—or not. It meant doing our most to persuade and encourage them, without drilling it home or boxing them in with hard, tight logic. Corralling someone with a well-crafted argument, or putting a God-trip on them, is no great achievement, and it is ethically dubious. At some point we are no longer ministering and persuading. We are simply overwhelming others into compliance. We are drowning them. We operate on the assumption that God is looking for a free, clean response from people, so we attempt to minister "cleanly" and honor their full freedom to make that response.

Spiritual leadership exercises pastoral oversight over people and manages the church and its ministries. We believe such authority stops short of micromanaging people's lives because that is the role of the Holy Spirit. To push it further is not simply intrusive, it is spiritually invasive. We read no suggestion in Scripture that God, when he places us in Christian fellowships under pastoral care and oversight, is farming out his children and the personal work of the Holy Spirit to spiritual subcontractors.

The End of the Story

I am Pentecostal. That means I am proud of my history and have a history of being proud. My generation in their youth enjoyed the euphoria of envisioning ourselves the front line in God's Kingdom too. With a tract in one hand, we went after everybody. We were doctrinally postured against the Baptists, who we acknowledged to be God's children too, yet lower on Jacob's ladder than ourselves. A "Charismatic nun" was still a confusing concept and what God was doing in their circles was initially a disturbing realization to many Pentecostals. We were at war with the Jehovah's Witnesses, the Children of God, and some of the religious eccentrics on the streets of downtown Edmonton. And we were leery of some of those Jesus People too.

When we are proud, Christ is no longer the measure of all things. We are, and we recast everything, almost unconsciously, in terms of "us" and "them." We go vertically and horizontally with the "us-and-them" approach—vertically with those of our own camp, imagining ourselves of a higher spiritual status than even our close associates, and horizontally with those outside the group, dismissing them as less enlightened and much less led of the Spirit than ourselves. Pride locks us in, then locks us down. It shrinks our spiritual world, closing us in around ourselves. We were sectarian and elitist to the core. That was us, my generation of youthful zealots—and that is a large cross-section of the contemporary Pentecostal-Charismatic world.

"Me against my brother. My brother and I against the world." That is a good description of many Pentecostal-Charismatics. It is an Arabic proverb, and it is true of them too. The difference, I think, is they know it is true of them. But I am not convinced we see ourselves that way.

When pride is driving us, we devise theologies to define our special place in redemptive history and comb the Scriptures to legitimize our lofty view of ourselves. We cannot help but see in the Bible that we are front and center in the Kingdom of God. Then we feed this back to ourselves and imagine that God himself is confirming those things to us. We look for deeper spiritual meanings in Scripture because the Bible's plain language would never endorse what we are imagining about ourselves or tolerate our "disqualification" of those who do not believe us. And we always find that special "light" we are looking for.

One can speak of personality cults and Charismatic churches that are "cultic," but the one that trumps them all is the cult of leadership. Leadership in the Pentecostal-Charismatic world is deeply in love with itself and has been from the earliest years. Leadership has become its own idol, and is constantly polishing and adoring the image it sees in the mirror. It has become its own end, ever defining and redefining itself and everyone else's place in the Kingdom of God. Leadership, in several Pentecostal-Charismatic sectors, effectively displaces the Holy Spirit as the main driver. And most of the errors and theological turbulence I have observed in the past forty years not only have derived from leadership, but they have fed it and pumped it up to new heights. Pentecostal-Charismatic leadership is obsessed with itself.

God's latest "new thing" in the Pentecostal-Charismatic orb is always the same old theological gaming under the hood. It is predictably a new cover of an old Pentecostal song. When I pull back the veils and unravel the spiritual spin in which it is wrapped, I always miss the "deeper truth" and "fuller light" that is in there. But I do see a little horn boasting great things. I see something with which I have long been acquainted and intimately know. I see collective Pentecostal-Charismatic pride in a clerical collar and wearing his Sunday suit.

Bibliography

Alley, J. Kingsley. *Holy Community: Experiencing the Grace and Purpose of Pentecost*. Rockhampton, Australia: Peace Publishing, 2010.

_____. *The Apostolic Revelation: The Reformation of the Church*. Rockhampton, Australia: Peace Publishing, 2002.

Blomgren, David K. *A Biblical View of Restoration*. Portland, Oregon: Bible Press, 1980.

Crosby, Stephen. *Authority, Accountability and the Apostolic Movement*. Enumclaw, Wa: Pleasant Word, 2006.

Fee, Gordon and Stuart, Douglas. *How to Read the Bible for All It's Worth*. Grand Rapids: Zondervan Publishing House, 1982.

Hamon, Bill. *Apostles, Prophets and the Coming Moves of God: God's End-Time Plans for His Church and Planet Earth*. Shippensburg, Pa: Destiny Image Publishers, 1997.

Hassan, Steven. *Combating Cult Mind Control*. Rochester, Vermont: Park Street Press, 1988.

Henrichsen, Walter A. *A Layman's Guide to Interpreting the Bible*. Grand Rapids: Zondervan Publishing House, 1978.

Hinchcliff, A. M. *Sons and Sonship*. North Battleford, SK: Sharon Children's Homes and Schools, 1999.

Holdcroft, L. Thomas. "The New Order of the Latter Rain." *Pneuma: The Journal of the Society for Pentecostal Studies 2(2)*.

Johnson, David and VanVonderen, Jeff. *The Subtle Power of Spiritual Abuse*. Minneapolis: Bethany House Publishers, 1991.

Michelsen, A. Berkely. *Interpreting the Bible*. Grand Rapids: Eerdmans Publishing House, 1963.

O'Connor, Edward D., C.S.C. *The Pentecostal Movement in the Catholic Church*. Toronto: Ave Maria Press, 1971.

Ruby, Lionel and Yarber, Robert E. *The Art of Making Sense: A Guide to Logical Thinking*. Toronto: J. B. Lippincott Company, 1974.

Sproul, R. C. *Knowing Scripture*. Downers Grove: Intervarsity Press, 1977.

Stott, John W. *Understanding the Bible*. Grand Rapids: Zondervan Publishing House, 1976.

Truscott, Graham. *The Power of His Presence – The Restoration of the Tabernacle of David*. Burbank, California: World MAP Press.

Wagner, C. Peter. *Apostles Today: Biblical Government for Biblical Power*. Bloomington, Mn: Chosen Books, 2006

Warnock, George H. *The Feast of Tabernacles: The Hope of the Church*. North Battleford, SK: Sharon Schools, 1978.

Yoder, Perry B. *Toward Understanding the Bible*. Newton, Kansas: Faith and Life Press, 1978.

CPSIA information can be obtained
at www.ICGtesting.com
Printed in the USA
LVOW04s1232241115

463888LV00016B/110/P